LONDON-

LONDON

SYDNEY

PHILIP J. BIRTLES

IAN ALLAN Publishing

Contents

First published 1993

ISBN 0 7110 2213 5

© Philip J. Birtles 1993

Published by Ian Allan Ltd, Shepperton, Surrey; and printed by Ian Allan Printing Ltd at their works at Coombelands in Runnymede, England.

Front cover:
The dramatic lines of Sydney's famous Opera House. *Australian Tourist Commission*

Front cover (inset):
The sleek lines of a BA 747-400. *Austin J. Brown/Aviation Picture Library*

Back cover, top:
The controls of a Boeing 747-400.

Back cover, bottom:
A BA 747-400 on the ground at Sydney. *Andrew Briggs*

Author's Note

A book of this nature can only be produced with the help of the many people involved in the operation of the aircraft. Allan Solloway and his public relations team at British Airways very kindly arranged the flight to and from Sydney, all the arrangements going very smoothly. The excellent help of all the aircrew and cabin crew was much appreciated. They all went out of their way to explain the many activities of operating the Boeing 747-400 to ensure the best possible coverage. We were made most welcome and had full access at all times.

It is always important to have the operational material correct, and Peter Hopwood, a pilot for British Aerospace, kindly agreed to check the relevant chapters and made some very helpful corrections. Tom Cole, the Public Relations Manager at Boeing, has always been supportive and, once again, supplied background material for this publication. On our departure from Sydney, I met Andrew Briggs on the roof of the terminal building and he agreed to help with the photos of the BA 747-400s in the Sydney scene, for which I am also grateful.

Finally, I would like to thank my wife, Martha, for helping with the photographs, particularly when I was busy taking copious notes, and for putting the transcript on to the PC.

Philip J. Birtles
Stevenage, May 1993

Above:
The Boeing 747-200, in service with British Airways, brought long-range high-density operations to the overall route structure including services from Britain to Australia. *Boeing*

Previous page:
British Airway's 747-400 G-BNLC pictured on final approach to Heathrow. *BA*

All photos by Martha and Philip Birtles unless otherwise credited

1. Air Route Development

The 9,750 mile journey by air from London to Sydney has not always been the routine it is today on the well-established airways of the world. It is still amongst the longest journeys possible by air with an elapsed time approaching 24hr. But 80 years ago the origins of the route lay in the development of improved transport links between various parts of the then British Empire.

Following the advance made in the reliability of aircraft and their operation during World War 1, it was possible to contemplate flying some of the longer distance air routes around the world. Whilst the crossing of the North Atlantic was a major barrier due to the great expanse of ocean, the flight half way round the world to Australia was more demanding on men and machines due to the range of climates from the cold of the Alps, the deserts of the Middle East and Australia, the jungles of Asia and the unpredictable seas from Singapore to Darwin.

Investigatory flights were being made from Britain to India in late 1918, when suitable longer range aircraft were freed from the hostilities of World War 1. Another significant step was the start on 25 August 1919 of the world's first scheduled daily international airline service from Hounslow Heath, close to today's London Heathrow, to Paris Le Bourget.

In November 1919, two brothers, Capt Ross Smith and Lt Keith Smith, departed from Hounslow in a World War 1 surplus Vickers Vimy bomber, powered by a pair of Rolls-Royce Eagle engines, to make the first flight from England to Australia. It took almost a month to fly the 11,290 miles (18,170km) to Darwin. What made the flight more demanding was the general lack of established facilities. Not only did suitable landing areas have to be found in parts of the world unfamiliar with aviation, but all the support services, particularly fuel, were also required. There were no established channels of spare parts and the aircraft would have needed continuous maintenance to ensure successful completion of the journey. Navigation would be somewhat basic and knowledge of hazardous weather would be sparse. Communications would be by Morse code if there was anyone to answer who could provide information of any value.

Although the subject of this story is an aircraft

Alan Cobham was knighted for his services to aviation following his epic route proving flight from Britain to Australia and back in a de Havilland DH50J . On his return on 1 October 1926, he landed on the River Thames. *BAe*

operated by British Airways, the London-Sydney route cannot ignore the efforts by the Australian-based Queensland and Northern Territory Aerial Service, known better today as Qantas. The airline was formed in November 1920 and started scheduled domestic services two years later.

Back halfway round the world in Britain, Imperial Airways became the country's first national airline in March 1924, combining together a group of the existing established companies. The first service under the new banner was flown between London and Paris on 28 April 1924.

To try and establish a basis for regular commercial flights to Australia, the well-known test pilot and enthusiast for aviation, Alan Cobham, with his engineer, A. Elliott, took Sir Sefton Brancker, the very active Director of Civil Aviation, on a series of long-distance survey flights. The first one was in a DH50 from London to Rangoon and back during the period from late January to mid-March 1924. A further survey flight, this time all the way to Australia and back, was flown by Cobham and Elliott in the DH50 from 30 June to 1 October 1926. Although aviation was becoming a little more familiar along the route, it still took a great deal of planning and was by no means easy. Alan Cobham did a great deal to popularise flying and the establishment of municipal airports around Britain. He later formed the Flight Refuelling Co, which pioneered air-to-air refuelling of aircraft.

As a result of the success of the survey flights, for which the pilot was knighted, Imperial Airways commenced proving flights with 14-seat DH66 Hercules aircraft. In December 1926, the first aircraft left Croydon for Cairo. These aircraft were to be used on the Cairo-Karachi route. A link was provided between Cairo and Port Said, where passengers travelled by sea to Marseilles. From Marseilles the passengers often travelled by train through Europe. Direct flights on one aircraft were unheard of at this time. Another development was the introduction by Imperial Airways of the 'Silver Wing' luxury service in May 1927. This service provided lunch on the London-Paris service. Today, it is rare to have time for any meal service on a short flight like London-Paris, but sustenance is now standard on most longer routes.

In March 1929, Imperial Airways inaugurated commercial passenger services from Croydon to Karachi. The journey took seven days and used progressively along the route the Armstrong Whitworth Argosy, Short Calcutta flying boat and DH66 Hercules. The gap was beginning to close.

However, the route still provided a challenge. On 7 February 1928, Bert Hinkler departed from Croydon in an Avro Avian to make the first solo flight from Britain to Australia. He arrived at Darwin on 22 February after flying over 11,000 miles (17,700km). Two years later, Amy Johnson left Croydon on 5 May in de Havilland Gypsy Moth, *Jason*. She arrived at Darwin on 24 May to become the first woman solo pilot to reach Australia. Although these solo flights did not represent commercial aviation, they did show that

Using a pair of de Havilland DH61 Giant Moths, Qantas commenced the first leg of the Melbourne to London air mail service on 4 April 1931. *BAe*

aircraft reliability was improving significantly. The major challenge was now the pilot's endurance.

As a further step towards a commercial aviation link between the two countries, Qantas Empire Airways was registered in January 1934. This company combined, in equal shares, the interests of Qantas and Imperial Airways. The major purpose was to operate the Singapore-Brisbane sector of the England-Australia route. As part of this plan the first Qantas international airliner, a four-engined de Havilland DH86 left Croydon on 24 September 1934 for delivery to Brisbane, where it arrived on 13 October ready to commence regular operations.

A major international event, in October 1934,

Right:
When Imperial Airways commenced services from Britain towards the connecting flights to Australia, both aircraft and facilities were somewhat rudimentary. In the de Havilland DH66 Hercules — an aircraft provided with the security of three engines — the pilot sat in an open cockpit above the passenger cabin. *BAe*

Below:
The winning MacRobertson Air Race de Havilland DH88 Comet Racer at Mildenhall prior to its departure in October 1934. Although the performance of the aircraft was excellent, it really had very little commercial application. *C. England*

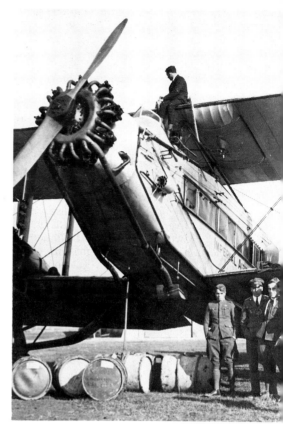

was the first great intercontinental air race, sponsored by Sir MacPherson Robertson, to celebrate the Centenary of Melbourne. Known as the MacRobertson race, the course was 11,333 miles (18,240km) long with five mandatory stopping points at Baghdad, Allahabad, Singapore, Port Darwin and Charleville. The start was Mildenhall in Suffolk and the finish was over the Melbourne racecourse in Victoria. Although about 70 aircraft were entered, 20 started and only nine finished the course. The race started at 06.30hr on 20 October, and the speed winners were C. W. A. Scott and T. Campbell Black flying one of the three specially-produced long-range de Havilland Comet Racers. This aircraft arrived after a gruelling 70hr 54min 18sec, representing an average speed of 158.9mph (255.7km/h). However, a significant winner in the handicap section, which came in close behind the Comet Racer, was a KLM-operated Douglas DC-2 airliner. This helped to point the way to practical commercial aviation.

With commercial aviation now a possibility between Britain and Australia, a regular weekly airmail service was inaugurated on 8 December 1934. Carrying air mail was less demanding than passengers, but did allow a practical proving of the concept. The London-Karachi section was operated by Imperial Airways, Karachi-Singapore was shared with Indian Trans-Continental Airways, and the Singapore-Brisbane leg was flown by Qantas. As a result of the success of this operation, Imperial Airways and Qantas opened the London-Brisbane route to passengers, the first through passenger flight leaving London on 20 April 1935. The first Australia-England passenger air service left Brisbane on 17 April. In May, the following year, the service was increased to twice weekly.

To bring long-range comfort to the service, the next major development was the introduction into service by Imperial Airways of the Short C Class flying boats. The initial operation was between Alexandria and Brindisi, but the type introduced a definite glamour to long-range aviation with a relaxed and comfortable flight and night stops at top-class hotels in exotic places. In early 1937, the C Class flying boat service was extended from Alexandria to Southampton on the final leg of the India to Britain route. In December 1937, Imperial Airways made the first flying boat survey flight from Britain to Australia, and then New Zealand, using a C Class flying boat.

Representing the epic long distance endurance flights mainly by de Havilland Moth variants, was DH80A Puss Moth flown by C. J. Melrose in the London-Melbourne MacRobertson Air Race. Leaving Mildenhall on 20 October 1934, this aircraft came third in the handicap section at an average speed of 103mph. *Aeroplane*

To support this activity from Australia, Qantas took delivery of the first of their C Class flying boats. The first aircraft departed from Southampton in March 1938. On 5 July, Qantas inaugurated operation of its C Class flying boats from Rose Bay in Sydney Harbour to Southampton Water in Britain, taking a total elapsed time of nine and a half days.

The declaration of war with Germany, in September 1939, put a stop to these developing routes, and reduced drastically the Empire air routes. With Italy and Japan also joining the hostilities, direct air links were closed down apart from essential military transport operations. Although not significant at the time, Imperial Airways and the domestic British Airways merged, in November 1939, to become BOAC (British Overseas Airways Corporation).

With the cessation of hostilities, BOAC and Qantas began a joint weekly service between Hurn airport, near Bournemouth, and Sydney Mascot, using Lancastrian aircraft. This was a passenger conversion of the famous Lancaster bomber. These aircraft were noisy and cramped,

and were unable to fly above the weather. In the Lancastrian it took a few days to complete the journey. The comfort levels were improved with the reintroduction of the C Class flying boats from Sydney to Singapore in October 1945 and, at the end of January 1946, BOAC resumed flying boat services from Britain to Singapore.

With the opening of London Heathrow on 31 May 1946, the death knell of the flying boat services was signalled. During World War 2, the USA had concentrated much of their efforts on transport aircraft, providing a ready fleet of commercial airliners to take advantage of the need for air communications worldwide with the coming of relative peace. Douglas had developed the DC-3 line into a progressively larger four-engined DC-4, through to the DC-6 and finally the DC-7C — the ultimate in piston-engined transports. Lockheed also produced the sleek line of the Constellation family. This type was also developed to its ultimate capability. Qantas operated the first through service from Sydney to Heathrow by Constellation on 1 December 1947. It was joined soon after by BOAC. The

Constellations took four days flying between London and Sydney with stops at Cairo and Singapore. BOAC finally withdrew their flying boat services on 7 November 1950, thus ending a romantic era in aviation.

With the arrival into service of these more modern and reliable long-range aircraft, the operations of BOAC and Qantas became largely independent. This introduced a more competitive operation over the Britain-Australia air route. This, of course, helped to improve the service to the passengers. In 1947, the Australian government bought out the BOAC 50% shareholding in Qantas and then nationalised the airline as a government corporation.

A major pioneering step in October 1952 was the introduction of the world's first commercial jet airliner — the de Havilland Comet — on the London Heathrow-Singapore route. This brought new levels of comfort with a lack of vibration, cruising above the weather, and faster journey times. Unfortunately, the early Comets were introduced before the full implications were understood with the result that several early aircraft were lost. It was not until the development of the improved Comet 4 that the aircraft could be reintroduced on the Singapore route in June 1959. Qantas commenced pure jet operations from Sydney to London, via the Pacific Ocean and USA, using Boeing 707s in September 1959 and, two months later, BOAC introduced the Comet 4 on the traditional London-Sydney route. Although Qantas never ordered Comet 4s, the airline operated some under lease from BOAC with its titles on the roof of the aircraft. In March 1965, Qantas introduced the Boeing 707-338C on the traditional scheduled 'Kangaroo' route to the UK.

In 1968 BOAC ordered its first Boeing 747s and, in 1973, the first 747-200Bs entered service with Qantas. The new British Airways was formed in 1972, by merging the operations of BOAC and BEA (British European Airways) and fully integrated operations were started on 1 April 1974. In February 1987, the state owned airline was privatised and now has a strategy of becoming a global operator by gaining major shareholdings in a number of other airlines worldwide.

Nowadays, it is the Boeing 747 'Jumbo' jet which flies the routes pioneered by the Vimy bomber. The 747 is operated by both British Airways and Qantas. It is interesting that, after some 45 years of independent operations between Britain and Australia, British Airways recently bought a 25% interest in Qantas, in preparation for privatisation of the airline by the Australian government. This will bring the advantages of combining much of the logistics of the two airlines.

The latest version of the 'Jumbo' is the 747-400, which first flew in April 1988. The main external difference of the new model is the wing-tip mounted winglets. However, internally, the systems have been considerably updated allowing a two-crew operation and many other sophisticated additions to the aircraft. Much of this latest operational technology will be revealed in subsequent chapters.

Latest version of the Jumbo Jet to enter the British Airways' fleet is the Boeing 747-400, identified by its winglets at the wingtips. *BA*

2. BA 011 Preparation for Departure

Although it is normal for the passengers to check in about two hours before departure on a long-haul flight, the crew are expected to meet for their briefing one hour before departure. This is the point where their duty period commences.

The Boeing 747-400 is normally operated by two members of the crew: the captain and usually a senior first officer. However, on the longer flights, such as London-Singapore, where flight time is over 12hr, a second crew is carried. The primary team is known as the 'operating crew' and the back-up team is known as the 'heavy crew'. It is normal for the operating crew to fly the aircraft for the first five or six hours, while the heavy crew rest, and then there is a change for about five hours, while the heavy crew take over. This gives an opportunity for the operating crew to rest and, for this purpose, a double bunk cabin is located just behind the flightdeck. With about an hour to go before arrival at the destination, the refreshed operating crew return to the controls for the descent and landing at the destination.

Although the operating captain is overall in command of the particular flight, the operation of the aircraft is a team effort and, at the pre-flight briefing, they all join together to discuss the route, the weather, any alternate airfields and any other aspects of the flight. Modern sophisticated aircraft can fly in most weather conditions, but there are always some which are best avoided for the safety of the aircraft and passengers. Therefore, any storm warnings will be taken very seriously. The crew will also select the best routing, if they have a choice, to achieve the most economical altitude, depending upon the aircraft loading.

The weather charts for BA 011 present fairly good conditions over Europe with a cold front curving around across Greece and Southern Europe. Clear air turbulence can be predicted, but the initial part of the route appears devoid of that phenomena which usually comes along just in time to spill the coffee. There are, however, warnings of isolated thunderstorms north and south of track of the proposed route over southeast Europe, while more are predicted over India and in the general area around Malaysia and our initial destination of Singapore. The route weather forecast also gives wind speed and direction and air temperature at flight levels 300, 340 and 390, these being equivalent to 30,000ft, 34,000ft and 39,000ft. Depending upon the altitude flown, outside air temperature will vary from a cool minus 30° C to a very sharp minus 60° C. Winds over much of the route were going to help the flight on its way, being generally favourable, but there were expected to be light winds against us over the Malaysian peninsular. Any predicted clear air turbulence appears well away from our flight 011.

A comprehensive briefing summary is presented to the captain for flight BA 011 on a 10-page computer printout, together with another 10-page printout giving up-to-date local weather at all the *en route* airfields and alternates. The weather for departure, given at 09.50 GMT is wind from 200° at 10kt, excellent visibility (9999 — known as all the nines), 1 octa cumulus at 2,000ft, 6 octa strato cumulus 4,000ft, temperature +13° C, dew point +09, pressure 1,013 and no significant change expected within the period.

The aircraft is on Stand V (for Victor) 20, the ETD (estimated time of departure) is 12.00 and the take-off slot of 12.22 is confirmed.

The briefing summary, with its 10 pages, appears to be hardly a summary, but it is the duty of the crew to read through it in order to highlight those aspects which will be applicable to this flight. Night jet movements at Heathrow will not apply for this flight. However, navigational aids, which are unserviceable or switched off for maintenance and which might affect the flight, need to be known. Any maintenance on the aprons and taxiways could affect the route out to the runway, and new push back and taxi out procedures from Terminal 4 must be checked to ensure BA 011 complies.

Weather at Singapore appears generally good with wind at 040°, 10kt, all the nines, 1 octa cumulus 1,800ft, 3 octas cumulus at 2,000ft, but there is a possibility of some thunderstorms in the area. The maintenance programmes at Singapore-Changi are noted as are any parking bays that are closed.

Alternative airfields for Singapore are what is known as 'overhead alternates', as they are flown over *en route*. If, due to weather problems or for any other operational reason, Singapore is

The operating crew and heavy crew gather for their briefing at flight operations. Left to right are: Senior First Officer Philip Morley and Capt Arthur Johnson of the heavy crew; and Capt Paul Grenet and Senior First Officer Nigel Golding of the operating crew.

not available for landing, one of the *en route* alternates is used. The alternates for this flight are Kuala-Subang in Malaysia or Bangkok-Don Muang. However, Kuala-Subang is not ideal as the control tower has been destroyed by fire and communications are severely restricted. Air traffic control at the airport was being handled by the air force tower on the other side of the runway and the new frequencies for radar, tower and ground were noted on the briefing. The airfield could still be used as a No 1 alternate for Singapore if a diversion was considered unlikely, otherwise Bangkok should be regarded as No 1 alternate. Meanwhile, the Bangkok weather was satisfactory, although the visibility was not as good.

Next the briefing summary lists special navigation warnings and notes along the general route, including any active danger areas. One of the cautions was over Yugoslavia where an unknown source on 133.45 was known to give bogus ATC instructions. Also for flights over the Adriatic Sea, north of latitude 40° N a listening watch must be kept on the international distress frequency of 121.5. Romania had imposed route restrictions affecting all overflights, and all flights overflying Bulgaria are instructed to contact the appropriate air control centre (ACC) at least 10min prior to reaching the Flight Information Region (FIR) boundary.

Flights over Iran are closely controlled along specific routes and once again crews are asked to monitor 121.5 within Iranian airspace. If a distress call is made and not picked up by any ACC, then it is the responsibility of the aircraft

picking up the signal to note and relay the details to an appropriate authority. Bahrain, Oman and Pakistan all require listening watch on 121.5, the information required being aircraft call sign, transponder code, heading, altitude and ground speed.

The flight plan supplied consists of 20 pages of computer printout. This is transmitted down the route to all major points, as well as the destination, and will be followed up on take-off with a confirmed departure signal.

Page one identifies the flight number, route, departure time and date, aircraft type and registration. The fuel plan is also listed and provides a total of 163,000kg. The fuel plan consists of the basic trip amount, plus contingency, diversion, reserves making up the required fuel, plus an allowance of 1,300kg for taxi to the take-off point.

The overall route will be over Germany, Czechoslovakia, Romania, Turkey, Iran, Karachi, north of Bombay, Calcutta, Rangoon, Phuket, Kuala Lumpur and Singapore. The latter part of the flight plan lists the latitude and longitude of the waypoints for the inertial navigation system, identifying the way point and giving the forecast winds at flight levels 290, 330, 370 and 410.

The pilots for this flight to Singapore are Capt Paul Grenet and Senior First Officer Nigel Gold-

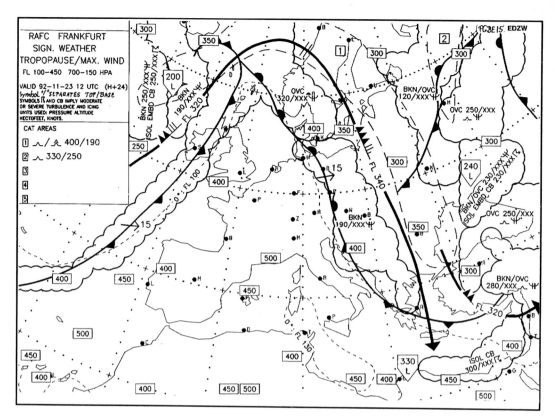

RAFC FRANKFURT
SIGN. WEATHER
TROPOPAUSE/MAX. WIND
FL 100-450 700-150 HPA

VALID 92-11-23 12 UTC (H+24)
Symbol "/" SEPARATES TOP/BASE
SYMBOLS Ƙ AND CB IMPLY MODERATE
OR SEVERE TURBULENCE AND ICING
UNITS USED: PRESSURE ALTITUDE
HECTOFEET, KNOTS.

CAT AREAS
1 ∧/ℛ 400/190
2 ∧ 330/250
3
4
5

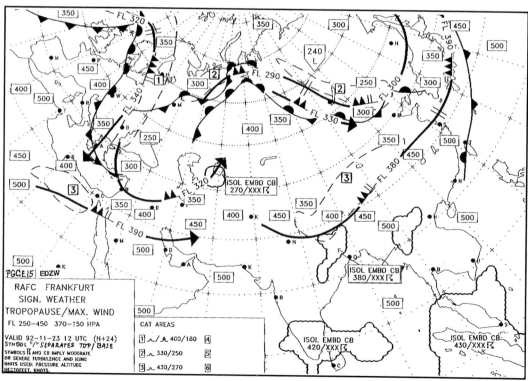

RAFC FRANKFURT
SIGN. WEATHER
TROPOPAUSE/MAX. WIND
FL 250-450 370-150 HPA

VALID 92-11-23 12 UTC (H+24)
SYMBOL "/" SEPARATES TOP/BASE
SYMBOLS Ƙ AND CB IMPLY MODERATE
OR SEVERE TURBULENCE AND ICING
UNITS USED: PRESSURE ALTITUDE
HECTOFEET, KNOTS.

CAT AREAS
1 ∧/ℛ 400/180   4
2 ∧ 330/250   5
3 ∧ 430/270   6

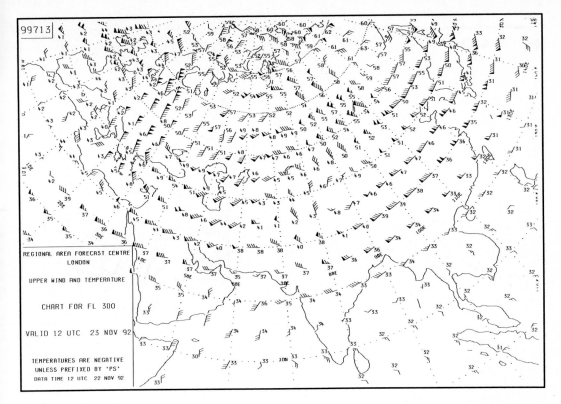

REGIONAL AREA FORECAST CENTRE
LONDON

UPPER WIND AND TEMPERATURE

CHART FOR FL 300

VALID 12 UTC 23 NOV 92

TEMPERATURES ARE NEGATIVE
UNLESS PREFIXED BY 'PS'
DATA TIME 12 UTC 22 NOV 92

Above left:
The European weather map for the flight of BA 747-400, G-BNLW, *en route* to Singapore, giving generally good conditions.

Left:
The route weather map from London to Singapore: the main hazard is isolated thunderstorms around Malaysia and Singapore.

Above:
The upper wind and temperature forecast for flight level 300.

ing, as the operating crew, and Capt Arthur Johnson and Senior First Officer Philip Morley, as the heavy crew.

Now that the briefing is complete, it is time to pick up the crew bus to be taken to the aircraft. In this case BA 011 is at stand V20, one of those which is still under construction in the easterly *cul de sac* behind Terminal 4. One routine check is to ensure the crew are boarding their nominated aircraft as it would be embarrassing to fly 385 eager passengers to the wrong destination.

Both the captain and the first officer need to make certain numbers of take-off and landings over set periods to maintain their currency. This is particularly difficult to achieve on the long-haul routes, where flying hours are plentiful but landings are hard to come by. To be qualified to make a flight, it may be necessary for a crew member to operate the flight simulator if he had not made a landing within the last 28 days. For the same reason, automatic landings are only made when it is necessary, since only manual landings keep the pilot qualified.

On arrival at the aircraft the crew split their duties between internal and external checks. A pilot seen walking round the outside of the aircraft does not mean he cannot find the way in, and it is not true that the captain does the walk round in good weather and the first officer in the rain. The usual routine is that whoever will be flying the aircraft on the route, that is the take-off and landing, will complete the external checks and the other crew member will cover the cockpit checks.

The external checks for today's flight are made by Philip Morley, the heavy crew senior first officer, while his two colleagues on the operating crew look after the flight deck. To anyone familiar with flying, the external checks tend to be a similar standard on any aircraft, but the scale is somewhat different from a Cessna 150 to a Boeing 747. The aircraft has been delivered to its stand after being checked by the engineering organisation but, in the unlikely event that something has been missed, an extra check

Philip Morley checks the nose-wheel tyres for any cuts and examines the undercarriage for any leaks on 747-400 G-BNLW.

Below:
With the forward hold loaded, the container hoist is ready to move away from the aircraft.

Right:
Philip Morley checks one of the main wheel undercarriage units for hydraulic leaks and tyre wear.

Below:
The final containers are loaded into the rear cargo hold as the aircraft is prepared for departure.

is always worthwhile, particularly by one of the crew responsible for the aircraft operation.

The walk round starts with a check of the static plates, providing outside pressure to the altimeters and the adjacent pitot tubes giving airspeed indication. During the entire walk round the external surfaces are being checked for damage which may have been caused by bird strike, lightning strike, foreign object damage (FOD) or damage from any ground servicing vehicle. The walk round includes the nose undercarriage where the tyres are checked for any cuts, the brakes for any undue wear, and the oleos for correct compression or leaks. The tyres generally have creep marks painted from the tyre wall to the wheel rim to ensure there has not been any creep which could pull out the air valve.

The structure is checked around the forward cargo door and along the wing leading edge to the tip, checking the engine cowlings and fastenings, as well as the front of the engine fan. The checks then continue down the wing trailing edge, including the engine jet pipes to the starboard main undercarriage. As with the nose wheels, the tyres, brakes and oleos are carefully inspected. The walk round continues down the starboard side of the fuselage, including around the rear cargo bay door and checking any other access hatches to make sure they are secure. The tail towers above the tarmac, and although a long way up, can be checked for any bird strike damage. As similar checks are made down the port side, the refuelling truck is just disconnecting from the wing and the last of the baggage and cargo containers are being stowed in the massive underfloor holds. Just as the walk round is completed the first of the passengers are arriving in buses and climbing the steps into the aircraft.

Meanwhile, all around, other aircraft are coming and going, and service vehicles are bustling about on their routine. Each aircraft type is designed to allow all the servicing vehicles to have access as and when required, the starboard doors opposite to the passenger entry being service doors for the loading and unloading of the catering, at the same time giving clearance for the special loading vehicles for the cargo containers. Pressure refuelling is metered out of underground pipes into the port wing where the fuel contents are controlled, allocating fuel to the various integral fuel tank zones within the wings, centre section and tailplane.

Meanwhile, the operating crew, Capt Paul Grenet and Senior First Officer Nigel Golding, assisted by Capt Arthur Johnson, have been running through the cockpit checks. For the overall systems checks, the on-board computers combined with the EFIS displays can be used for determining serviceability. Each check is called up on the EFIS and has to be satisfied before moving on to the next item. As only two crew operate the aircraft, the flight engineer duties have been built into the computers, but there are four seats on the flightdeck — the captain on the left, the first officer on the right, a rear starboard seat which can be positioned centrally behind the pilots as an additional systems monitor and the fourth seat over on the left behind the captain. The primary flight instruments are duplicated for both pilots to allow either to fly the aircraft, and the communications and systems are centrally located and are accessible to both pilots. Generally, the communications and navigation controls are located on a central console between the pilots and the aircraft systems such as air-conditioning, fuel flow, electrics, etc are mounted above the pilots in the cockpit roof. Additional controls on the central panel are for the engines including thrust levers, starting and fuel cocks, plus trims for the flying surfaces. These areas will be dealt with in more detail later, as they affect operation of the aircraft.

While Capt Arthur Johnson is liaising with the senior members of the cabin crew on behalf of Capt Paul Grenet to ensure every eventuality is catered for, the operating crew are preparing the aircraft for departure. This is probably one of the most intense periods of activity for the crew, since all actions need to be completed satisfactorily in the relatively short time to departure.

If, on arrival in the cockpit, the ground engineering team have not turned on the aircraft electrical and air supply, this is the first duty of the operating crew. A safety check is made to ensure the hydraulic pump selectors are off, the landing gear lever is selected down and the flap position indicator and flap lever position selector agree. This avoids an embarrassing incident when power is selected. The auxiliary power unit (APU) is then started. The APU is a small turbine engine located in the rear end of the tail cone, which exhausts to the rear. With this unit running, electrical power is established for the aircraft systems, including cabin lights and air conditioning to either warm or cool the cabin, whichever is the most appropriate for the local climate. On the flightdeck the three inertial reference systems (IRS) are selected to navigation mode (NAV).

It is always good practice for the crew to complete a security check of the flightdeck area to ensure that no suspicious items, such as explosive devices, have been smuggled aboard. A loose equipment list is checked, covering the

Right:
The front fan of the Rolls-Royce RB211 is checked for foreign object damage. The spiral on the centre spinner is believed to discourage birds, which are a regular hazard to jet engines.

Below:
A recognition feature of the Boeing 747-400 is the wing-tip mounted winglet, which is visible here as Philip Morley checks the wing trailing edge.

Left:
Whilst the Boeing 747-400 tail towers above the apron it still has to be checked for any visual foreign object damage.

Right:
With G-BNLW, *City of Norwich*, nearly ready for departure, the fuel pump wagon is ready to pull away from loading the aircraft tanks from underground piped supply.

Below right:
The passengers board at the unfinished stand V20 at London Heathrow.

safe stowage of emergency equipment, such as fire axe, smoke hood, portable oxygen bottles, torch and first aid kit. The ship's library has to be checked to ensure that all the mandatory manuals, such as flight manual and documents, such as certificate of air worthiness (C of A) and insurance certificates, are present. The library also includes a range of reference instruction manuals to be used to assist in trouble shooting should a fault occur.

The cockpit pre-flight systems and equipment check, known as the scan check, is started once the crew members have settled into their seats and strapped in. The procedure is employed to check every item on the flightdeck and its correct operation. The scan check begins at the top left hand side of the overhead engineering and systems panel, working down past the circuit breaker panel and covering the overhead systems panel, selecting the relevant electrical, hydraulic and fuel systems to the appropriate

setting in preparation for start up. The autopilot mode selection is checked along the glare shield above the main instrument panel, and then the engine parameters on the cathode ray tube Engine Indicating and Crew Alerting System (EICAS) screens in the centre of the main panel.

Moving back on the console between the pilots, the parking brake is on, the speed brake in, thrust levers (previously known as throttles) closed, the flap lever and trim positions are selected and noted. The relevant frequencies are set on the radios and navigation equipment and the aircraft's current position is inserted into the appropriate page of the master control display unit (MCDU), by keying in the four letters EGLL, identifying London Heathrow. The windscreen heaters are switched on, not just for demist or, in cold climates, to de-ice, but to avoid brittleness caused by low temperatures. The airliner windscreen has to contain the pressurisation loads from within and the possibility of bird strike from outside. It, therefore, consists of a number of layers of toughened glass with acrylic sandwich and an integral gold film heating element to comply with stringent structural and safety requirements. The operation of the evacuation alarm system is checked.

The first officer begins the scan of his own panels on the right of the cockpit, starting with the side wall, the electronic flight instrument system (EFIS) source selection at the panel's edge, down the primary flying display (PFO) and navigation display (ND), over the lower EICAS checking the status display and finishing at the MCDU of his flight management system (FMS). The old analogue instrumentation has largely been replaced by cathode ray tubes (CRT) on the Boeing 747-400, although analogue instruments are still used for standby. The primary flight, navigation and systems information can all be selected on the CRTs, giving clear displays in colour with no parallax in all outside lighting conditions. These CRTs offer more information, are more reliable and compact than the earlier

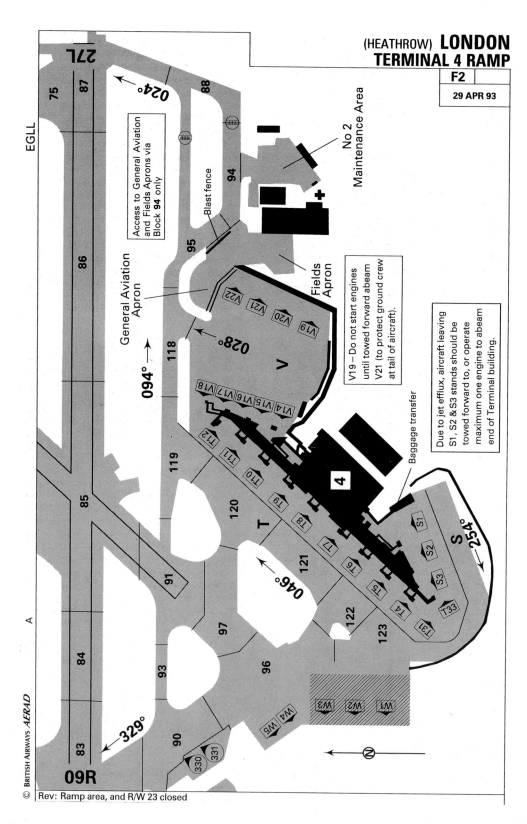

(HEATHROW) LONDON
TERMINAL 4 RAMP

F2

29 APR 93

EGLL

27L

No 2 Maintenance Area

Access to General Aviation and Fields Aprons via Block 94 only

Blast fence

General Aviation Apron

Fields Apron

V19 – Do not start engines until towed forward abeam V21 (to protect ground crew at tail of aircraft).

Due to jet efflux, aircraft leaving S1, S2 & S3 stands should be towed forward to, or operate maximum one engine to abeam end of Terminal building.

Baggage transfer

094°

028°

024°

046°

254°

329°

09R

Stands: V22 V21 V20 V19, V18 V17 V16 V15 V14, T12 T11 T10 T9 T8 T7 T6 T5 T4, T33 T31, S1 S2 S3, W1 W2 W3 W4 W5, 330 331

4

T

S

© BRITISH AIRWAYS AERAD

Rev: Ramp area, and R/W 23 closed

traditional instruments, and even the CRTs will soon be displaced by even more compact and lighter liquid crystal displays on the next generation of commercial aircraft.

With the flightdeck checks complete and everything required for the safe operation of the aircraft serviceable, the crew can now commence the procedures for departure. Although the aim is always to operate with everything serviceable, there are a number of allowable deficiencies, which can be carried over to a next maintenance check, either due to lack of time on the ground or non-availability of parts. Modern aircraft carry a high level of systems redundancy to ensure safe operation, and not all systems are essential all the time.

The first officer selects the air traffic information service (ATIS) frequency of 133.07, to copy the actual weather conditions. Information 'LIMA' is currently being broadcast, giving wind 210°, 17kt, temperature +13°C, QNH 1,013mb and runway in use 27R. The QNH of 1,013 is today, in effect, close to the International Standard Atmosphere based on mean sea level, which is the pressure setting used by all aircraft altimeters when flying above the normal *en route* transition altitude of 3,000ft. This ensures adequate separation between aircraft flying at different flight levels, on a variety of headings.

Using this information and knowing the total weight of the aircraft at 390 tonnes, the first officer can calculate the critical take off velocities of V_1, at 157kt, V_R 170kt and V_2 180kt. V_1 is the critical go or no-go decision speed on the runway. In the event that an emergency occurs prior to reaching V_1, there is sufficient runway available to safely bring the aircraft to a halt. V_1 is the most critical at weights approaching the maximum, where high energy braking action can cause brake overheating, burst tyres and possible runway over-run. At lower weights, V_1 is much less critical, but runway conditions need to be considered, as only a certain amount of water is allowed to be present. Our take-off today is from a dry runway. V_R, the rotation speed, is the take-off velocity at which the pilot pulls back on the control column, raising the nose to the take-off and climb out position. The aircraft then leaves the runway for its climb out. V_2 is the safe climb out speed in the event of the loss of an engine at V_1. Normal climb out is at V_2 + 10kt.

Left:
The AERAD chart of Terminal 4 at London Heathrow shows the position of Stand V20 on V Apron adjacent to Fields. Boeing 747-400 G-BNLW taxied from V along blocks 118, 119, to 91 and crossed runway 27L at block 85.

If the aircraft is under maximum take-off weight, to preserve engine life and reduce fuel consumption, something less than maximum power can be selected, depending on runway length, temperature, wind speed and direction and any other meteorological or operational factors. The correct take-off power, using all the parameters, is calculated with the aircraft computer, using an assumed temperature of 44°C.

The captain completes his own panel check, ensuring that all the equipment and systems are functioning correctly, and checks the instrument departure procedures. He then loads the FMC with required routing, including the take-off flap setting of 20°, the information being cross-checked with the first officer to avoid errors. Although departure clearance is not issued until engine start is required the runway in use has already been identified from ATIS and the standard instrument departure (SID) required for the routing can be planned in advance. In today's case, a left turn will be made after take-off, to Epsom, routing to Detling and Dover. By the time the aircraft is over Detling, it will be at 6,000ft, awaiting its next altitude clearance.

The captain discusses the emergency procedures with the first officer, running through the checklist and agreeing actions throughout the full range of possible emergencies which could occur. He asks for all crew members on the flightdeck to watch out and advise in case there is something happening of which he is unaware. In his emergency procedures briefing, the captain asks the first officer to announce any malfunctions, the captain then decides whether to stop or continue. Up to V_1 any fire or engine failure indicated by two or more parameters would mean abandoning the take-off. If either crew member calls stop, the captain will close the thrust levers and apply maximum braking, although these are normally applied automatically with auto rejected take-off brakes armed. Maximum available and symmetrical reverse thrust was to be selected by the first officer and a check made that the speed brakes had automatically deployed. In the event of an engine failure, reverse thrust will not be available from this unit either, making it essential not to select too much reverse thrust on the opposite side. As the aircraft is coming to a halt, the captain will call for the appropriate Quick Reference Handbook (QRH) covering the emergency checklist.

For an emergency after V_1, the take-off continues and the first officer confirms safe climb away with undercarriage selected up. The captain will concentrate on flying the aircraft and communicating with the ground. When ready,

the captain will call for the appropriate QRH from the first officer. The first officer will make any adjustments, including engine shut down action monitored by the captain. It is, of course, important that the faulty engine is clearly identified before it is shut down. If a landing is necessary, a return will be made to Heathrow either immediately, if it is an emergency, or after reducing to the landing weight if only precautionary. The three-engine clean up height, which means flap retraction, is 1,080ft, allowing 1,000ft above the Heathrow elevation of 80ft, the safety height is 2,300ft and the transition altitude is 6,000ft, within the London control zone.

The fuel contents are checked, comparing the fuel loader's figures with the computer print out of the aircraft contents. Manual dip stick readings are no longer practical. With 154,000kg of fuel, which is 9,000kg below maximum, the fuel log is signed. The technical log is then checked for any unserviceabilities, signed by the senior ground engineer and then by the captain. The captain is now, in effect, accepting full command of the aircraft. The load sheet is checked and any dangerous goods are correctly and safely stowed. The main items are aerosols required for spraying the aircraft on arrival at Sydney to kill any undesirable insects. Listed under special loads is a live dog, located in the special live animal compartment where there is adequate temperature and pressure, and food and water available. The captain questions the need for any special documentation, but is assured that this is no longer required in Australia. The door check is selected on the EFIS display and shows all but one closed. When this is closed, the door selectors are changed from manual to automatic, the significance of this is that, in the unlikely event of an emergency evacuation, opening the doors will automatically

COCKPIT SAFETY CHECK

Battery Switch .... ON
Standby Power Switch .... AUTO
Hydraulic Demand Pumps .... OFF
Engine Start Switches .... IN
Windshield Wiper Switches .... OFF
Alternate Flap Selector .... OFF
Landing Gear Lever .... DOWN
Flap Position Indicator & Lever .... AGREE

CLEARED FOR START

Hyd Demand Pump No. 4 _____ AUX
Hyd Demand Pump No. 1 _____ AUX/AUTO
Autostart Switch _____ AS REQD
Fuel Load & Pumps _____ CHECKED & SET
Packs _____ ONE ON
Beacon _____ BOTH
Doors (Prior to pushback) _____ CLOSED

BEFORE START

Int/Ext Preparation _____ COMPLETED
Oxygen _____ CHECKED/100%
Flight Instruments _____ SET
QNH/Aa _____ SET/CROSSCHECKED
Park Brake _____ SET
Fuel Control Switches _____ CUTOFF
Autobrake _____ RTO
Passenger Signs _____ AS REQ'D

- - - - - - - - - - - - - - - - - - Briefing - - - - - - - - - - - - - - - - - -

AIS & DDM Items
Runway State - Significant Weather
Emergencies - Performance Restriction - Return Alt
SID - Radio Aids Set - AFDS (LNAV, VNAV, Hdg, Alt)
Terrain Clearance - Transition Altitude

- - - - - - - - - - - - - - - - Ships Papers - - - - - - - - - - - - - - -

FMC _____ LOADED
T/O EPR _____ SET
Ref Speeds _____ SET
LNAV/VNAV _____ AS REQD

AFTER START

APU Selector _____ AS REQD
Anti-ice _____ AS REQD
Aft Cargo Heat _____ AS REQD
Air Conditioning _____ SET
Recall _____ CHECKED
Gnd Eng Taxy Clearance _____ RECEIVED

BEFORE TAKE OFF

Vital Data _____ RELEVANT FOR RWY/LOADSHEET
Flaps _____ ( ) GREEN
Flight Controls _____ CHECKED
Trim _____ UNITS & ZERO
Transponder _____ SET
Cabin Crew _____ REPORT RECD

- - - - - - - - - - - - - Entering Runway - - - - - - - - - - - - -

Exterior Lights .... AS REQD
Cabin Crew .... SIGNAL

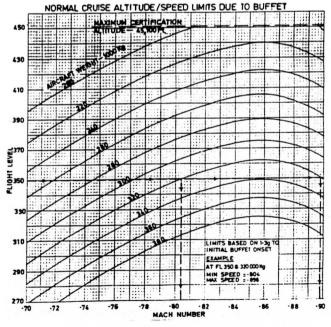

NORMAL CRUISE ALTITUDE/SPEED LIMITS DUE TO BUFFET

Obtain appropriate speed by reference to speed tape and/or IAS/MACH window on MCP

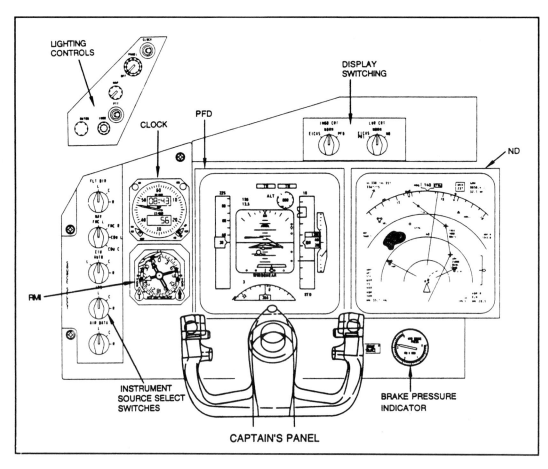

LIGHTING
CONTROLS

DISPLAY
SWITCHING

CLOCK

PFD

ND

RMI

INSTRUMENT
SOURCE SELECT
SWITCHES

BRAKE PRESSURE
INDICATOR

CAPTAIN'S PANEL

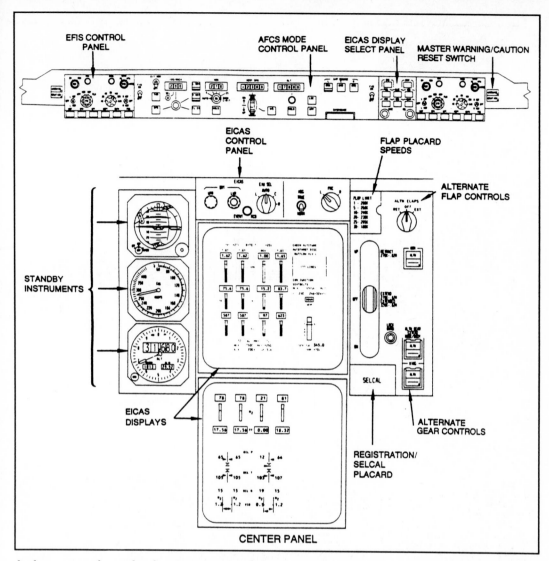

EFIS CONTROL PANEL

AFCS MODE CONTROL PANEL

EICAS DISPLAY SELECT PANEL

MASTER WARNING/CAUTION RESET SWITCH

EICAS CONTROL PANEL

FLAP PLACARD SPEEDS

ALTERNATE FLAP CONTROLS

STANDBY INSTRUMENTS

EICAS DISPLAYS

ALTERNATE GEAR CONTROLS

SELCAL

REGISTRATION/ SELCAL PLACARD

CENTER PANEL

deploy escape chutes for the passengers to slide down to get clear of the aircraft quickly.

The Before Start checks are completed, including oxygen at 100 per cent, flight instruments-set, QNH-set and passenger signs on auto. On the autopilot mode control panel the runway direction of 27 for take-off is set in the heading windows and the 6,000ft transition altitude is set in the altitude window, the aircraft climbing automatically to that height and levelling off, unless a further setting is selected. The lateral navigation (LNAV) and vertical navigation (VNAV) are checked armed. Climb-1, for econ-

omy, is selected on the computer for the required climb.

The call-sign of today's flight is Speedbird 011 identifying it as British Airways Flight Number BA 011. All the major airlines have their own company call-sign, which is sometimes the airline name, and, on other occasions, a special identity established with the operator. As long as there is no chance of confusion, then there is no problem.

Nigel Golding tunes the radio to 121.7 in preparation for request to start. He calls 'Speedbird One One, stand Victor 20 Information Lima request start for Singapore via Dover 2 Foxtrot, squawk 0312.'. The 'Cleared for Start' checks are run through including Hydraulic Demand Pump No 4 on auxiliary, Hydraulic Demand Pump

Left:
Capt Paul Grenet signs the technical log accepting the Boeing 747-400 from the maintenance crew.

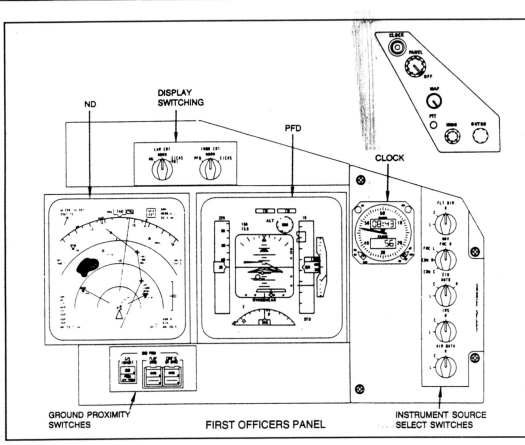

DISPLAY
SWITCHING

ND

PFD

CLOCK

GROUND PROXIMITY
SWITCHES

FIRST OFFICERS PANEL

INSTRUMENT SOURCE
SELECT SWITCHES

No 1 on auto, Fuel Load and Pumps — check and set, Packs — one on, Beacon — on, Doors — closed. Paul Grenet is talking via the intercom to the ground engineer by the nose of the aircraft to ensure the steps and ground power have been removed and that the tractor is ready to push-back the aircraft. Pre-start checks are complete and brakes released. Time is now very short to achieve the approved take-off slot, so, as Nigel changes to 121.9 and calls for push back, which is approved, Paul commences auto-start on engines Nos 3 and 4 under the starboard wing. This is a new feature of the Boeing 747-400 which allows automatic engine start by computer control, to overcome some of the problems which could occur on manual starts. Time is also saved by starting two at a time.

As an additional point, the two reference points on an aircraft are the nose and the left, or port, wing tip. The captain always sits in the left-hand seat (unless the aircraft is a helicopter), and therefore in a multi-engined aircraft, No 1 engine is always the port outer. The seat rows in the cabin are numbered from the front and, with the letter designation across the cabin, A is always on the port side. It is always best to refer to port or starboard, as they are fixed in relation to the aircraft forward direction, where as left or right depends which way you are facing. The port wing-tip displays a red light and the starboard wing-tip a green light.

Once in the centre of the apron and clear behind, Nos 1 and 2 engines are put on auto-start and the engines spool up to idle power. The ground engineer calls brakes to park, confirms undercarriage locks removed and signs off by exiting left and giving thumbs-up to the captain.

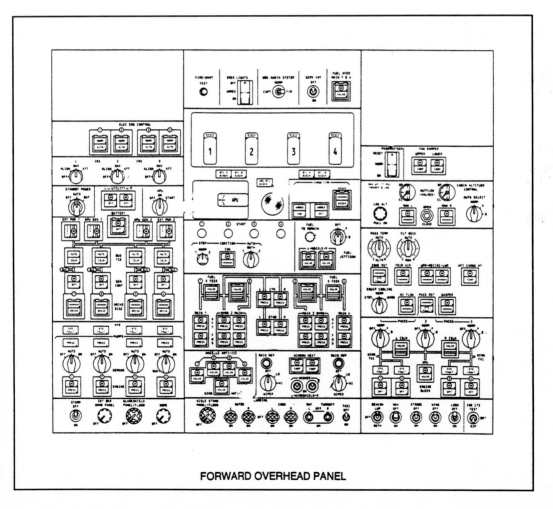

FORWARD OVERHEAD PANEL

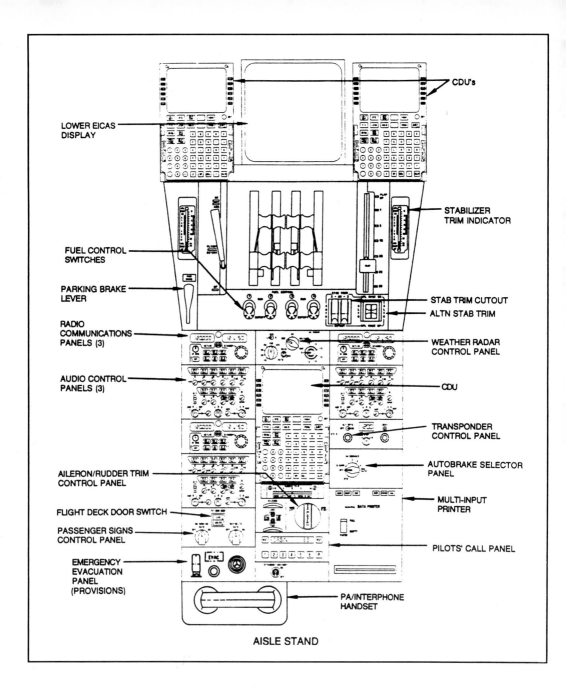

CDU's

LOWER EICAS DISPLAY

STABILIZER TRIM INDICATOR

FUEL CONTROL SWITCHES

PARKING BRAKE LEVER

STAB TRIM CUTOUT

ALTN STAB TRIM

RADIO COMMUNICATIONS PANELS (3)

WEATHER RADAR CONTROL PANEL

AUDIO CONTROL PANELS (3)

CDU

TRANSPONDER CONTROL PANEL

AILERON/RUDDER TRIM CONTROL PANEL

AUTOBRAKE SELECTOR PANEL

FLIGHT DECK DOOR SWITCH

MULTI-INPUT PRINTER

PASSENGER SIGNS CONTROL PANEL

PILOTS' CALL PANEL

EMERGENCY EVACUATION PANEL (PROVISIONS)

PA/INTERPHONE HANDSET

AISLE STAND

Above right:
As we push back, engines No 3 and 4 are started and running.

Right:
With all engines running and systems operating, the Boeing 747-400 taxies out towards the runway.

Above:
The Federal Express DC-10 held waiting to cross 27L.

Right:
After crossing 27L at block 85, we continue along the diagonal runway for the threshold of runway 27R.

The after-start checks are made, selecting the APU as required, Anti-ice — off, Aft Cargo Heat — on, Air Conditioning — set, Recall/Status — checked, FMC — updated, T/O EPR — set, Ref Speeds — set, LNAV/VNAV as required.

Air traffic control passes the taxi clearance which is read back by Nigel 'One One Victor, left on Southern block 91 for 27 Right, crossing 27 left'. We commence rolling at 12.15hr and the pre take-off checks are started. Vital data is checked as relevant, flaps are set at 20°, flight controls are checked on the computer, trim is set as required, transponder is checked as set and the cabin crew report is received, that all the passengers are settled in.

Speedbird 11 is then held on block 91, turning to the right with a Federal Express DC-10 also holding ahead waiting to cross 27L when it is clear of traffic. Radio tuned to 118.7 'Speedbird One One after landing United 767 expedite crossing 27L, continue straight ahead and change to tower 118.5 for departure'. Nigel acknowledges the instructions and changes to 118.5 as we cross the runway in parallel with the Fed Ex DC-10. We join the line of aircraft

with four ahead awaiting departure, Speedbird One One being just behind the cargo DC-10.

Air traffic call 'Clear line up 27R' which Nigel responds, identifying us as 'Speedbird One One', and pre take-off checks are completed with confirmation of clearance to the transition altitude of 6,000ft on QNH 1,013. The tower then calls 'Speedbird One One, clear take-off, 27 Right, Wind 240 20,' and Nigel responds 'Clear take-off 27 Right, Speedbird One One'. Paul eases the power levers forward as the aircraft begins its roll, the take-off being under automatic power, but pilot-operated flying controls, and soon after rotation he calls for gear-up, a change of frequency to 128.4 and we are airborne at 12.28, within the pre-planned time scale.

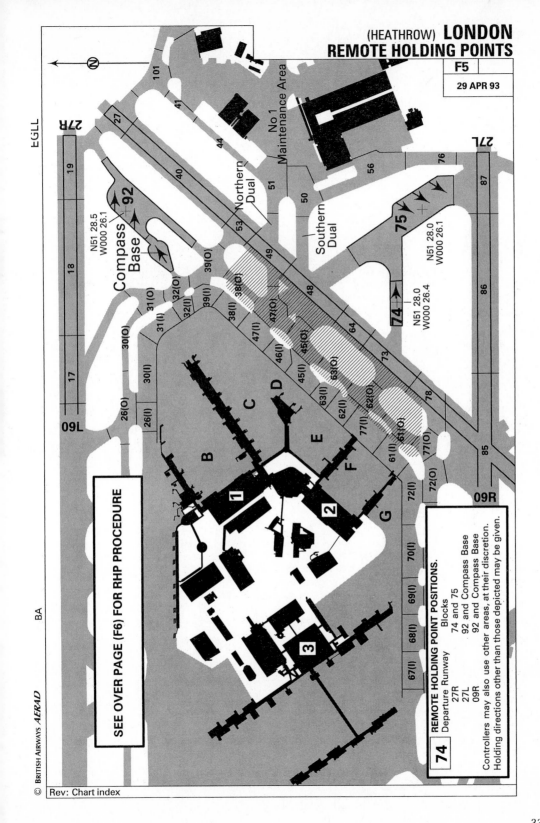

(HEATHROW) LONDON REMOTE HOLDING POINTS

F5

29 APR 93

No 1 Maintenance Area

Northern Dual

Southern Dual

Compass Base

N51 28.5 W000 26.1

N51 28.0 W000 26.1

N51 28.0 W000 26.4

27R

27L

09L

09R

EGLL

BRITISH AIRWAYS AERAD

BA

© Rev: Chart index

SEE OVER PAGE (F6) FOR RHP PROCEDURE

74	REMOTE HOLDING POINT POSITIONS.
Departure Runway	Blocks
27R	74 and 75
27L	92 and Compass Base
09R	92 and Compass Base

Controllers may also use other areas, at their discretion.
Holding directions other than those depicted may be given.

33

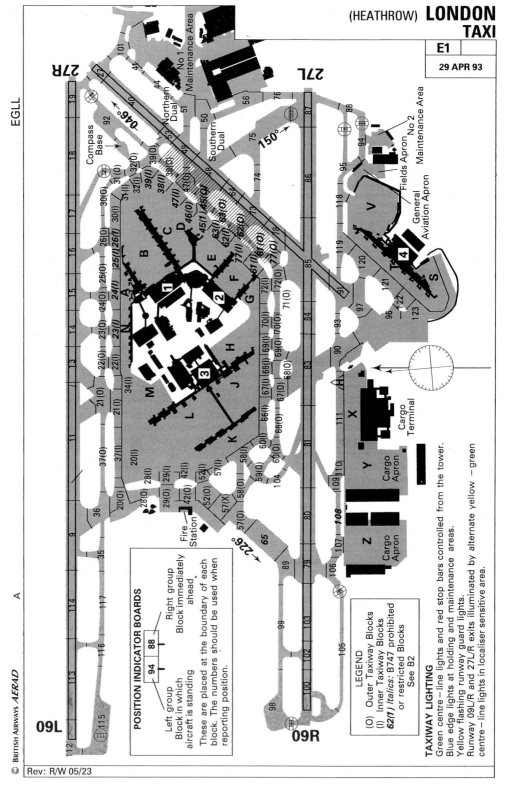

EGLL

27R
27L

No 1 Maintenance Area

Northern Dual
046°

Compass Base

Southern Dual

150°

No 2 Maintenance Area

Fields Apron

General Aviation Apron

V

4

S

T

Cargo Terminal

X

Y
Cargo Apron

Z
Cargo Apron

226°

Fire Station

B
C
D
E
F
G
A
N
M
L
K
J
H

1
2
3

09L
09R

226°

POSITION INDICATOR BOARDS

94	88

Left group
Block in which aircraft is standing

Right group
Block immediately ahead.

These are placed at the boundary of each block. The numbers should be used when reporting position.

LEGEND
(O) Outer Taxiway Blocks
(I) Inner Taxiway Blocks
62(1) Italics: B747 prohibited or restricted Blocks See B2

TAXIWAY LIGHTING
Green centre – line lights and red stop bars controlled from the tower.
Blue edge lights at holding and maintenance areas.
Yellow flashing runway guard lights.
Runway 09L/R and 27L/R exits illuminated by alternate yellow – green centre – line lights in localiser sensitive area.

BRITISH AIRWAYS *AERAD*

© Rev: R/W 05/23

34

Left:
The overall London Heathrow chart shows the layout of the four terminals, the cargo area, the maintenance area, the two main runways, and the rarely used for landing diagonal runway.

Above:
Cathay Pacific and Virgin Boeing 747s awaiting departure from runway 27R.

Right:
Capt Paul Grenet manoeuvres our Boeing 747-400 on to the runway.

Below:
The Federal Express DC-10 ready for departure moves forward to the threshold of Runway 27R.

3. BA 011 LHR-Singapore

'Speedbird one one, Dover departure, climb to 6,000, no air traffic speed restrictions,' comes from air traffic to our Jumbo jet as Nigel commences the stepped retraction of the flaps from 20° to 10°, five degrees and then fully up at 1,400ft, and the nose lowered slightly as the speed is increased. Climb rate is 800ft per minute and, with the flaps fully retracted, we break through the cloud layer at 4,000ft after four minutes airborne.

When the flaps had been raised to the five degree setting, the auto throttle, which had been monitoring the initial climb power, reduces to the CLIMB 1 power setting. The first officer confirms that the climb selection is indicated on the EICAS display and selects the landing gear lever to the off position. The lowering of the nose up attitude commanded by the auto pilot maintains the required climbing acceleration with reduced power. As the trailing-edge wing-flaps come to the fully up position, the outboard wing leading-edge flaps retract automatically. The inboard and mid-span leading-edge flaps are retracted at the same time, cleaning up the wing from its maximum lift configuration at take-off to its minimum drag shape for the economic cruise.

We turn on to a magnetic heading of 135° at 5,600ft and, as we continue to climb, the auto pilot levels us off at 6,000ft, until we are cleared to climb further on track.

The QNH is set at 1,013.2 on the altimeter at the transition height of 6,000ft in the London Terminal Movements Area (TMA) and the auto heading is dialled left on 095, then 085 to bring the aircraft on to computer track.

During the flap retraction between 10 and 5°, the fuel system is automatically reconfigured so that all available fuel in the tailplane, centre section and main inboard wing tanks is available to feed all the engines. As fuel is used up in the tailplane and centre section, making it even across the wing tanks, the system will be switched to each tank zone feeding its respective engine. As on all modern jet powered aircraft, the fuel is carried in integral tanks within the overall structure, suitably sealed against leaks occurring at the skin and structural joints. The wing ribs provide surge baffles and non-return valves to manage the distribution of the fuel. Fuel distribution is also an essential part of the balance and bending stresses of the aircraft.

At the transition altitude of 6,000ft the flight director horizontal bar indicates the attitude required to maintain the level, and the captain eases forward on the control column to avoid exceeding this cleared level. The thrust levers automatically reduce to maintain the correct speed. The captain then calls for the first officer to select autopilot and, as the engage button on the autopilot/flight director system (AFDS) is selected, the top of the primary flying display (PFD) shows the letters CMD to confirm the autopilot is in command. The LNAV, which is commanded just after take-off, continues to control progress, automatically guiding the aircraft on track. The aircraft is now flown through the autopilot, the next heading and altitude selections being made in the autopilot panel. When an alternative heading is required by air traffic control to avoid conflicting movements, the new heading is selected. This disengages the LNAV and the aircraft automatically banks to the new heading. To climb to the next cleared flight level, the height is dialled into the altitude window and, on selection, the aircraft climbs to the new level with climb power automatically applied. The aircraft also accelerates towards the most economical climb speed.

The radio is changed to 134.9 — London Radar — the heading being confirmed at 085 with a further climb clearance shortly. This then comes through as a clearance to climb to FL150 on a heading of 085. Heading is later given as 105° with clearance to climb to FL290. At this stage, we are coming up to overhead Dover at 18,000ft, a speed of 335kt/Mach 0.702 and the time is 12.42. The post take-off checks now need to be carried out to ensure nothing has been missed earlier. The first officer reads the items and carries out the actions monitored by the captain. The landing gear is checked selected to OFF, the flaps are checked up, the air-conditioning is checked as set, and the engine nacelle anti-ice is checked in auto. There is a risk of ice forming at temperatures below 10°C in visible

Right:
Dover departure chart: Speedbird one one departed from runway 27R, turning left after take-off to overhead Detling and then Dover.

	G4	
	04 MAR 93	

Trans Alt **6000**

1. Initial climb: Ahead to 580. **2.** Callsign for RTF frequency use when instructed after take – off 'London Control'. **3.** On initial contact with London Control, include callsign, SID designator and current altitude/flight level. **4.** En – route cruising level will be given by London Control after take – off. **5.** Max 250kt below FL100 unless otherwise authorised.
6. Cross Noise Monitoring Terminals at or above 1080, thereafter maintain min gradient of 4% (243'/nm) to 4000. See C1.

EGLL

G/S kt	100	130	160	190	220	250	
ft/min	410	530	650	770	890	1010	243'/nm

NOT TO SCALE

DVR 3L

LON 113.6 · LON 1.3d · LON 2d · 098R · 119R · 214R · LON 2d · 27L MM · 135R · LON 4d

DVR 3K

DET 28d **3000 or above**

25nm

DET 20d **5000 or above**

DET 16d **at 6000**

DET 5d **at 6000**

DETLING DET 117.3
N51 18·2
E000 35·9

125° · 125° · 110° · 108°

143° · 153°

DVR 2F,2G · DVR 2H · DVR 3J

Biggin BIG 115.1

30
111°

DOVER DVR 114.95
N51 09·7
E001 21·7

← DET 276R → · 096°

EPSOM 'EPM' 316
N51 19·1
W000 22·2

above 3000

DET 30d **5000 or above**

Abm BIG DET 21d **at 6000**

DET 5d **at 6000**

DVR 2F,2G,2H

SSA 25nm

2₂	2₃
2₁	2₃

AVERAGE TRACK MILEAGE TO DET	
DVR 2F	50
DVR 2G	49
DVR 2H	47
DVR 3J/3K	41
DVR 3L	42

SID	R/W	ROUTEING(including Min Noise Routeing)	ALTITUDES
DVR 2F 128.4	27R	At 09L MM left on 'EPM' 143M to 'EPM'. At 'EPM' left on Tr096M(DET 276R) (but not before LON 10d) to DET then right on Tr111M(DVR 291R) to DVR.	'EPM' above 3000 DET 30d 5000 or above DET 21d (Abm BIG) at 6000 DET 5d at 6000
DVR 2G 128.4	27L	At LON 214R/2d left on 'EPM' 143M to 'EPM'. At 'EPM' left on Tr096M(DET 276R) (but not before LON 10d) to DET then right on Tr111M(DVR 291R) to DVR.	
DVR 2H 128.4	23	Ahead to intercept 'EPM' 153M to 'EPM'. At 'EPM' left on Tr096M(DET 276R) (but not before LON 10d) to DET then right on Tr111M(DVR 291R) to DVR.	
DVR 3J 128.4	09R	At 27L MM (LON 135R/2d) right onto Hdg 125M. At LON 4d left on Tr108M(DET 288R) to DET then right on Tr111M(DVR 291R) to DVR.	DET 28d 3000 or above DET 20d 5000 or above DET 16d at 6000 DET 5d at 6000
DVR 3K 128.4	09L	At LON 119R/1.3d right onto Hdg 125M. At LON 4d left on Tr108M(DET 288R) to DET then right on Tr 111M(DVR 291R) to DVR.	
DVR 3L 128.4	05	At LON 098R/2d right to intercept Tr110M(DET 290R) to DET(LON 110R) then right on Tr111M(DVR 291R) to DVR.	

A

Rev: Editorial

Chart H203 shows joining airway UG1 at Dover *en route* to Sprimont, Nattenheim and Frankfurt. The flight then followed UA 19 towards Cheb on entering the Prague FIR. Airway UA17 was flown to Brno, and then UA4 to Nitra and Rutol before leaving this chart east of Vienna.

moisture, such as cloud. Automatic ice sensing detectors operate hot-air bleed from the engine compressors, to feed slots in the engine intakes to prevent ice forming. Therefore, in potential icing conditions, the cowls are kept free of ice accretion. A build-up of ice could break off and cause engine damage by ingestion into the fan blades. Ice can also form on the airframe, the wing leading edges being the most vulnerable. This causes loss of lift and a dramatic increase in drag. It is avoided by channelling hot air, controlled from the cockpit, along the leading edges. The post take-off checks are confirmed complete.

London Radar advises the crew to operate on their own navigation systems and call Maastricht on 132.2 which gives clearance to restrict climb to FL210 on 132.85, with the reporting point of Koksy, estimated at 12.48. A clearance

is given to climb to FL330, but the captain responds negative due to being too heavy at this stage and is given the flight level of 290. Meanwhile the navigation computer is advising that our estimated time of arrival (ETA) at Singapore is 00.43 GMT the next day and the fuel remaining will be 31 tonnes.

With the aircraft cleared to 'own navigation', the autopilot takes over fully, selecting the next waypoint into the FMS by the 'go direct' instruction to Konan, which is selected in the top of the route page and locked on by pressing the execute button. The flight log identifies the airway to be used, having joined UG1 at Dover, the identity and frequency of the VOR or equivalent beacon, the distance between each beacon, the time in minutes between each VOR and the cumulative time to landing at Singapore.

Climb rate is now 900ft per minute and overhead Kok we are passing through 25,000ft at a speed of 335kt/Mach 0.796, the Mach number increasing with altitude and the reducing air pressure/temperature as we climb. We were over Belgium at 12.50 and, after 25min in the air, we level off at 29,000ft; the T/C (top of climb) being indicated on the EFIS screen. Our speed is now 320kt with a Mach number of 0.836, close to our

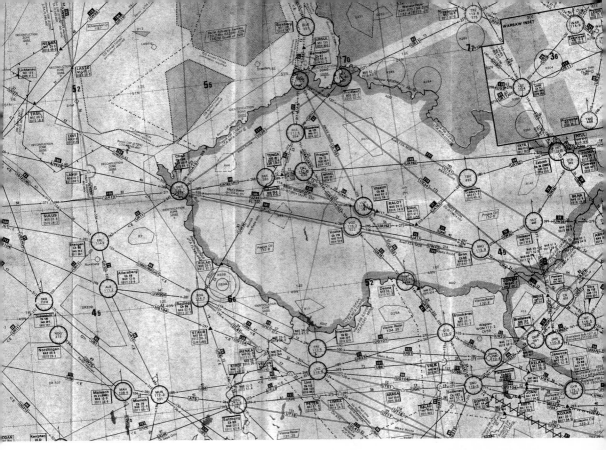

target maximum cruise of Mach 0.84. We call 'level at 290' on the RT. Our heading is 114°, track 111° with a strong tailwind component, the wind bearing 253° at 48kt. Our ground speed is 532kt and we have used 10.9 tonnes of fuel to reach the start of our cruise overhead Brussels.

The flight has now lapsed into the routine cruise after all the busy activity of the pre-flight checks, take-off and climb. The captain now has time to communicate with the passengers, who are beginning to enjoy their pre-lunch drinks.

'We are 50 miles east of Frankfurt and will be routing over East Germany, Czechoslovakia, Rumania, Istanbul in Turkey, Tehran in Iran, Karachi, India — north of Bombay, between Madras and Calcutta, over Phuket in Thailand, Kuala Lumpur in Malaysia and then landing at Singapore. We are currently at 29,000ft, climbing gradually to 33,000ft and eventually to 37,000ft. There are strong winds forecast of up to 170 miles per hour from the North and there may be some turbulence, so we suggest you stay strapped in while seated during the flight. The forecast is good with some showers in Asia and we expect to arrive at Singapore on the schedule at 00.23 hours GMT, landing at 09.05 hours local Singapore time. Enjoy your flight.'

Once leaving the control of Maastricht, TOK is top of climb position with a target Mach number of 0.84 and ground speed of 537kt, our actual being close to the flight planned predictions. During the climb the crew check the actual times with the predicted plan on their flight log, monitoring the performance of the aircraft to determine any major variations in the predicted arrival time. An early arrival is not always welcome, as it could be during a night time curfew or before slots are available for landing and parking. This could result in having to hold, or orbit, before landing which being at progressively lower levels uses up additional expensive fuel. It is, therefore, more economic to use less fuel by reducing power during the overall journey, taking advantage of the prevailing winds. Late arrival can be critical for the same reasons; and, therefore, on-time departures and arrivals are most desirable. If, for any reason, the flight departure is delayed beyond the time that would exceed the overall crew duty period, starting one hour before the planned take-off, a whole new crew would have to be located and brought to the aircraft. Such an occurrence is rare, but can happen if there is a major unserviceability or the weather deteriorates badly.

Above:
Climbing through 16,820ft, we have an indicated airspeed of 336kt and a heading of 101° magnetic as we approach the Dover overhead.

Below:
Chart H109 picks up at Nitra on airway UA4 to Dunakeszi, UG1 to Bekes, UA17 to Dombi, UT51 to Valpa, UA17 to Rixen where we enter the Istanbul FIR. We cross Turkish airspace, joining VG8 at Valova, leaving the top right hand corner of the chart after Elazig.

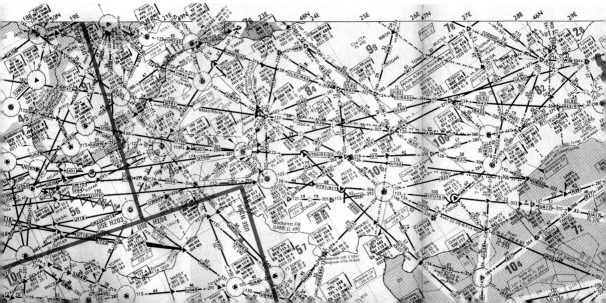

Clearing the control of Maastricht, we are requested to change to 129.52 Rhein as we reach Remba. We then change frequency to 132.32 under Rhein control for the next stages of the flight. The VORs at Navil, Sprimont, Lared and Nattenheim are passed when the Mach number reduced slightly to 0.839 and our ground speed is 533kt. Time is 13.06 and we change airway to UA19 at Frankfurt and are cleared direct Cheb on airway UA17 with an ETA of 13.32, our flight plan time being 1.03 at this point.

The captain continues to monitor the radio communications while the first officer manages the FMS. On arrival over Cheb, we call Bratislava on frequency 134.47 for continuing *en route* clearance to Vozice and Brno, where we change airway to become established on UA4 matching our ETA and ATA at 13.52 — within one minute of our fight planned time. We continue on airway UA4 via Hodon, Berva, Nitra and Rutol, where a time check shows we are still within one minute of the fight plan, and, after Sturovo, we call Budapest control on 126.5 as we pass overhead Ergom.

With the crew settled into the routine of the flight, the time is right to clarify many of the activities of the preparations and departure when many of the automatic actions were just a rapid blur of activity.

Although the flight plan is supplied by the British Airways flight operations, it is the crew's responsibility to ensure it is accurate and acceptable. There can be between 10 to 12 routes available for any one flight, the computer flight plan being the most economical available, perhaps saving between 3 and 4 tonnes of fuel. The crew also have to satisfy themselves that the planned fuel flight plan is adequate. Generally the supplied flight plan is about 95% accurate and, at the crew briefing, the combined sug-

gestions of the operating and heavy crews make the fine tuning to adjust for any variations in the standard parameters used by flight operations. Having looked at the flight plan together, any final decisions, as a result of the team effort, are the responsibility of the operating captain.

On our flight, the operating crew will fly for the first 5.5hr, the heavy crew then taking over for about six hours, allowing the operating crew to complete the final hour to landing at Singapore.

Because of the significant changes in airspeed with the increase in altitude, giving reduced pressure and temperature, the velocity of the aircraft is measured by a decimal fraction of the speed of sound, or the Mach number. The target Mach number for our flight is M 0.822, which is the most economical speed giving the best fuel consumption. The stalling speed of the aircraft varies with the weight, gravity forces, flap setting, altitude and a number of other less critical parameters. The FMS works out the band of safety of minimum and maximum speeds, which, in our case, is between 274 and 352kt. Our indicated airspeed is 319kt. As the altitude increases so the band of safety reduces. The altitude limiting speed restricts us to a maximum altitude of 35,100ft at the current weight of 338.7 tonnes.

The total operating cost benefit is measured against a cost index of 90. However, it is not easy to maintain the ideal Mach number as the airways routes are like three dimensional motorways and can be just as subject to congestion as a road system, but without the possibility of stopping in a service area. All aircraft want to be at their most economical height, which tends to be relatively common for all modern jet engines, and alternate flight levels are used for aircraft travelling in different directions along the speci-

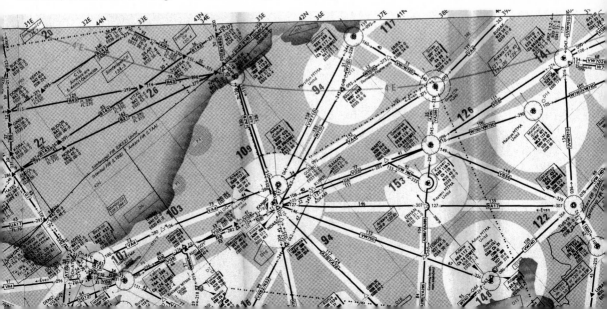

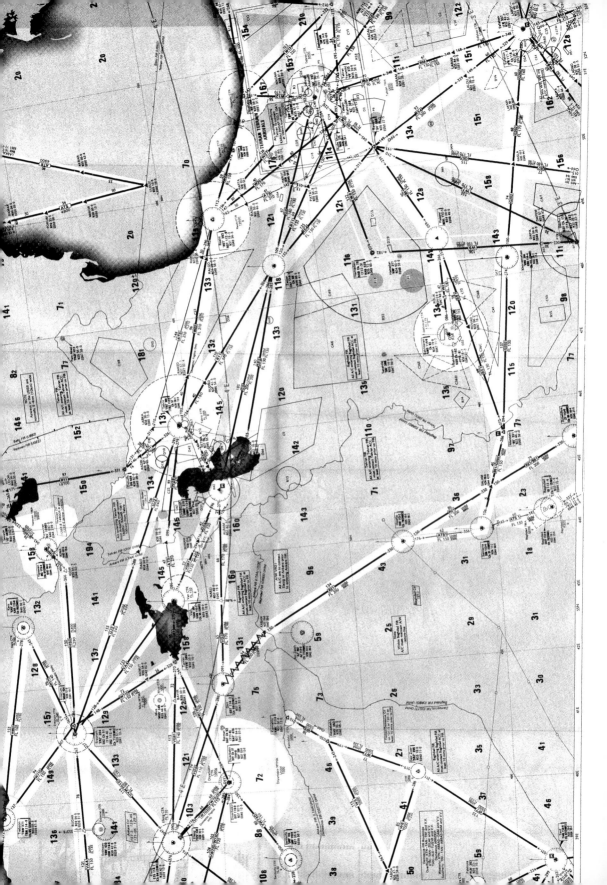

fied airway. There is also a 15 minute separation between each aircraft, so a slower one up front can hold up the entire line behind at that level. Equally, if an aircraft is catching up behind, it is sometimes necessary for the aircraft in front to increase speed slightly to maintain the required separation.

Our flight was 11min late on departure due to a breakdown of the computer which works out the load and balance sheet. On departure, we weighed a total of 386 tonnes, including 163 tonnes of fuel, 233 passengers, four flight deck crew and 18 cabin crew. The additional allowance of fuel for taxi to the holding point prior to departure was 1.25 tonnes. The massive holds were filled with containers holding the passenger luggage and additional commercial cargo, as well as all the catering and other items required for the passenger complement on the main deck.

As already mentioned the modern flightdeck of the Boeing 747-400 uses cathode-ray tube (CRT) instrument displays which give excellent colour clarity under all light conditions. This is the result of the automatic variation in brightness and also greater reliability.

The number one Electronic Flight Information System (EFIS) is known as the Primary Flying Display (PFD). On one screen is shown the artificial horizon which indicates the relative level of the wings in relation to the horizontal; the heading, which combined with the wind velocity component gives the actual track; the altitude above mean sea level assuming standard conditions so that all aircraft are using the same reference; the indicated airspeed; the Mach number; the vertical speed indicator, which in the cruise will be zero; and the turn and slip indicator which shows that the aircraft is in balance, particularly in a turn. Apart from the Mach number, all this information is displayed to the average private pilot in his light aircraft on the familiar analogue instruments. An additional piece of data on the PFD is the target information for the flight director.

Standby analogue instruments are fitted. These include an artificial horizon, air speed indicator, altimeter, direction finder, a clock which is an essential ingredient to navigation and an RMI.

The EFIS Navigation Display (ND) features a computer generated moving map display showing the aircraft in the form of a triangle or pure

Left:
On Chart ME1 we fly airway VG8 to Siirt and Narli north of Baghdad FIR. We follow G8 to Zanjan across Iran and R54 to Esfahan and off the chart towards Ladal.

delta. The aircraft position is shown on the map diagramatically, an example being overhead Ankara we check the track at 15.27 and are six miles to the right. The display gives the distance to the next waypoint and a curved line provides the compass bearing. Ground speed is noted at 518kt and the wind is on a bearing of 253° at 39kt. The radio navigation information such as VOR and DME is on the ND as required.

The single EFIS No 2 in the centre of the panel always displays the standard engine information including temperatures and speeds, any faults being shown automatically. A red alert on the central panel, plus an audible warning with the relevant information will signify an important fault, while amber is precautionary and green is routine. The central maintenance computer monitors all systems and provides a passive alert if anything malfunctions or becomes unserviceable. In addition, a flight data recorder (FDR) records all operational parameters to monitor overall performance and assist with the maintenance of the aircraft. Much of the latter can be on condition, rather than remove serviceable components before there is a need for repair or overhaul. Systems technology is now advancing to the stage where the FDR can download its information automatically on discrete frequencies to the operators central maintenance computer. As equipment, such as engines, begin to suffer loss of performance and become less efficient within certain tolerances, maintenance can be scheduled at the next convenient break to keep the aircraft in its most efficient condition.

Below the centre of the main instrument panel is a further EFIS display which takes over some of the previous work of the flight engineer, who used to be the third crew member. This display covers all the aircraft systems on eight pages, any of which can be called up by the crew to check faults. The computer itself is programmed to make any correction or adjustment, recording the unserviceability for repair on the ground. The crew are kept aware for information although there is nothing they can physically do to make any adjustments.

Page one covers the full engine parameters and operating conditions. Fan Speed N1 and Core Speed N2 are monitored with fuel flow, oil pressures, temperatures, quantity and vibration. It can be recorded as any of these parameters begin to approach the limits on their tolerances. Fuel flow is an obvious sign of efficiency as well as being a measure of the economy. Any excessive vibration will suggest that an engine is out of balance. This could also result in damage within the engine as well as inefficient running.

Page two gives a simplified diagram of the aircraft's electrical circuits, showing the four bus-bars off the engine driven generators, plus the power from the APU which can be run during flight if there is an electrical failure elsewhere, and also the electrical circuit from the ground power connector. In addition to these power sources, there are also batteries to provide essential power in an emergency.

Fuel management is on page three. This gives diagrammatically the capacity of the various tank zones, the status of the fuel pumps, whether they are on or off, and the total fuel contents at any one time.

Left:
Cruising through the night at 28,900ft at 310kt. The camera flash has blanked out the Efis displays. The heading is 135°.

Below:
Chart ASI/1, starting on airway R54 at Ladal, 'BA one one' flies R54 to Kerman and G52 to Zahedan. We enter Pakistani airspace on Airway G8E overhead Karachi, and cross into Indian airspace at Telem, the airway becoming G472 crossing Bodar *en route* to Dakos.

Page four, the Environmental Control System (ECS), controls the air conditioning in the cabins, measuring engine bleed air and operates the automatic anti-icing systems. It meters the airflow line to the air conditioning packs, controls pressurisation, notes temperature selected and when it is achieved. We noted that our travelling dog should have been warm enough at +21°C. One of the major problems caused by high altitude flight is the lack of natural water vapour and, therefore, dehydration over long periods of flight. Alcohol, of course, does not help at all, indeed makes the condition worse. Water is freely available on the aircraft and orange juice served by the cabin crew also helps keep the crew and passengers in a fitter state on arrival at the destination. Something else which is not widely known, is that it is an offence to be drunk on an aircraft, even as a passenger. Therefore, it is unwise to take too much advantage of the alcoholic hospitality.

The four-engine driven hydraulic systems are displayed on page five noting temperature, pressure and fluid quantities and showing which pumps are operating. Each system has to be capable of independent operation, so that the

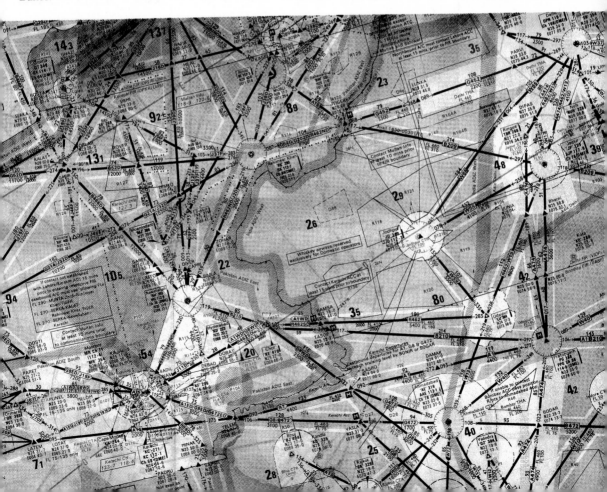

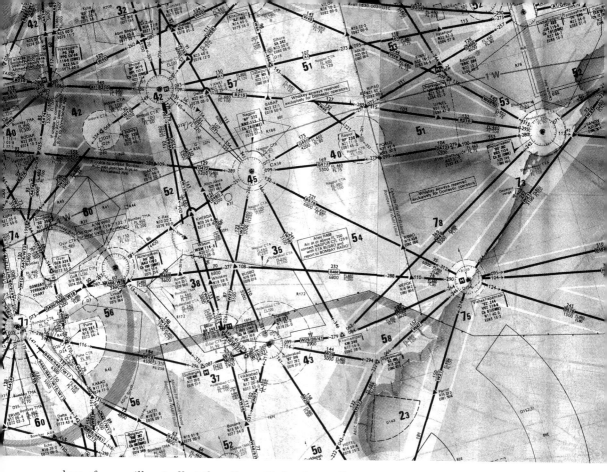

loss of one will not affect the others. Hydraulic power is essential for operating the controls of the aircraft, including the ailerons for lateral control, the elevators in the tail for longitudinal control and the rudder for directional control. Hydraulics also power the flaps on the wing trailing edges, which are deployed for take-off and landing to provide more lift at lower speeds, the wing leading-edge slats, which operate in conjunction with the flaps, the airbrakes and lift dump system (which create drag to slow the aircraft down), the engine thrust reverse systems to assist braking on landing, the wheel brakes and the undercarriage retraction and lowering. Without hydraulics, an aircraft is practically immobilised.

Information of use during the preparation for departure and after arrival are on page six, which gives a simple diagram of the aircraft cabin with all the door locations. It indicates when doors are either open or latched shut and, when they are closed, whether they are set in manual or automatic mode. Automatic is the normal condition for the aircraft from taxi out to stop. This is to facilitate the deployment of the escape slides as mentioned earlier.

Above:

On Chart ASI/2 we fly along G472 to Nagpur, changing to B579 to Vishakhapatnam where we commence our ocean crossing, over Port Blair and making our landfall at Phuket.

Right:

Flight 'BA one one' then flew down the Malaysian coast over Penang and Kuala Lumpur to Singapore.

Again provided mainly for use on the ground, approach to land and departure, is the undercarriage status which is given in a simple diagrammatic form with a plan view of the wheels and doors. These give tyre pressures, brake temperatures and undercarriage door positions. A high brake temperature is a 'no go' item, as they heat up quite considerably on landing, and must cool down to an acceptable level before departure. The long-haul airliners are not normally limited by this, but the quick-stop short-haul airliners make much greater use of their brakes and, thus, high brake temperature can be a problem.

The final page, eight, gives a general information status, particularly on the condition of the

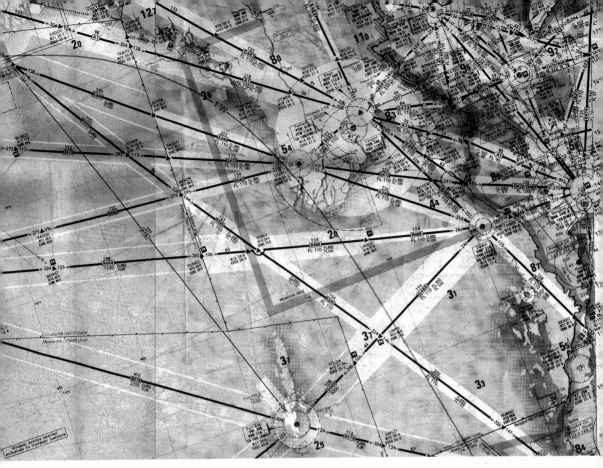

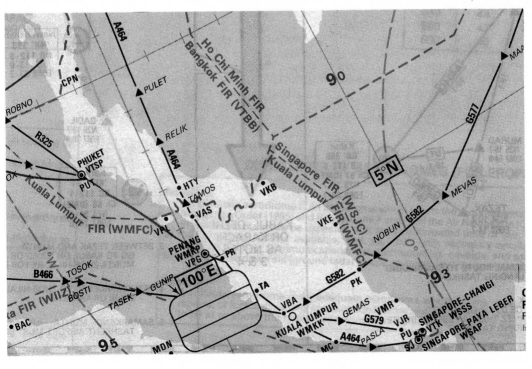

APU, as well as the position of the various controls. It can also be interrogated for the identification of any problems or faults, since it has room for the display of any systems malfunction not shown up on the simplified diagrams on the other pages.

Our flight continues in its routine. We change airways from UA4 at Dunakeszi to UG1 at Tapiosap, UA17 at Bekes and UT51 at Arad until we call Bucharest control at Varna on 125.7mH at 14.45. From Bucharest, we are handed over briefly to Istanbul on 119.3 on airway UA17 and change to Ankara on 128.8. We remain under the control of Ankara FIR for the next hour and a half, as night falls. Whilst we change frequencies overhead, we fly above the remote beacons below — beacons in some of the most barren areas of southeast Europe as it merges into the deserts of the Middle East. At Siirt, we are advised to call Tabriz radar on 134.1 10min prior to reaching Alram and we follow that with a call to Tehran on 125.7. Tehran controls our flight for the next 1,000nm. On changing to 123.9, still under Tehran's control at Bonik, we are cleared to FL330 after a Lufthansa aircraft ahead has turned off our airway R54 heading for Dubai. The time is 17.47, which is four minutes behind our plan, and we have been airborne for 5hr 19min. We increase our speed slightly to allow 15min separation from the aircraft behind when we reach overhead Karachi. We climb automatically to 33,000ft at 1,500ft

pipes all day or demolishing the bathroom in the room across the corridor. After a suitable rest period, Arthur and Philip, the heavy crew on our flight, will take a flight from Singapore to Perth, Western Australia, on their own. The flight crews can expect normally three nights at home before the next trip, although this can be extended for a number of reasons. The crews, who are rostered for about one month in advance, can bid for the preferred trips, the more popular ones being decided on seniority. If the preferred trips are generally achieved, then this allows more consistent planning of domestic activities, avoiding unnecessary friction at home.

The operating crew must remain alert during their duty time operating the aircraft, although there is very little to do apart from monitoring progress of the aircraft. We are flying well above the weather at a height of around five miles, so there is very little sensation of movement and the darkness outside is only broken by the flashing beacons of aircraft ahead, above and below.

The *en route* duties of the flight crew include updating the loading of the FMS, particularly with data on *en route* winds and temperatures. Systems monitoring is a continuous process, as is communications with air traffic control. It is, therefore, always important to maintain a continuous listening watch for other radio communications, because this can warn of a possible conflict with other aircraft. Two aircraft reporting at the same beacon at the same altitude and the same time can be generally regarded as unhealthy. This is one way of ensuring reasonable separation *en route* which is one of the main duties of the crew. Also, as the aircraft loses weight due to burning off fuel in the cruise, the crew need to obtain clearance to continue climbing to a more economical altitude, at the same time ensuring that there is no speed restriction due to slower traffic. The all-important cost factor is the main parameter, apart from safety, which guides the total operation of the aircraft. The crew need to maintain an awareness of the weather conditions at the destination, as well as the diversions, to allow planning well in advance. A regular check is maintained of the fuel programme to ensure sufficient reserves remain, which have not been eroded by any unforecast headwinds. The crew are continually communicating with the air traffic control units on both VHF and, in the more remote areas, using the rather more antiquated HF (high frequency) radio equipment. The navi-

per minute and a speed of M 0.85. To increase the speed, we increase the cost index to 330 and compare the results on the computer. As we climb a green curved line predicts our acquisition of achieving the set altitude.

We call 'Speedbird one one passing flight level 327, approaching 330'.

Our operating crew on this flight, Paul and Nigel, will complete their current duty in Singapore, where they will have two nights to rest before taking a 747-400 back to London. As the return flight will be overnight, their rest periods have to be adjusted to allow them to be as fresh as possible for the long dark flight back. This is not always easy as every hotel has its resident hammer operator who either is hitting adjacent

AFTER TAKEOFF

Landing Gear	UP & OFF
Flaps	UP
Air Conditioning	SET
Nacelle Anti-icing	AUTO

------------- Trans Altitude -------------

Altimeters	STD/CROSSCHECKED

DESCENT BRIEFING

Safety Altitudes - Trans Level
U/S Items - Sig Weather - Handling Pilot-
MAP integrity - STAR - Approach
Runway State - Reverse - Brakes
Airfield
Go-Around - Diversion

DESCENT/APPROACH

Recall	CHECKED
Briefing	CONFIRMED
V$_{REF}$	SET
Minima	SET

------------- Trans Level -------------

MAP Integrity	VERIFY
Altimeters	QNH/CROSSCHECKED

LANDING

Speedbrake	ARMED
Autobrake	SET
Landing Gear	DOWN
Flaps	( ) GREEN
Cabin Crew	REPORT RECD

AFTER LANDING

Strobes	OFF
Stabilizer	6 UNITS
Speedbrake	DOWN
Flaps	UP
APU Electrics	AVAIL

------------ Approaching Stand -----------

'Doors to Manual'	CALLED

SHUTDOWN

Hyd Demand Pumps	OFF
Fuel Pump Switches	OFF
Aft Cargo Heat	OFF
Wx Radar	OFF
Park Brake	AS REQUIRED
Fuel Control Switches	CUTOFF

SECURE

IRS	OFF
Emergency Exit Lights	OFF
Packs	OFF
Ext Power	ON
APU	OFF
Standby Power Switch	OFF
Battery Switch	OFF

V$_{REF}$ SPEED

V$_{REF}$ SPEED ADJUSTMENT:
+ 1 KT/4000 FT ABOVE S.L.

ADD WIND FACTOR OF:
1/2 HEADWIND COMPONENT
+ GUST (MAX: 20 KNOTS)

WEIGHT 1000 KG	KIAS	
	FLAPS	
	25	30
400	192	184
380	187	179
360	181	174
340	176	168
320	170	163
300	164	158
280	158	152
260	152	146
240	146	140
220	139	133
200	132	127

1 (2) ENGINE INOP
DRIFTDOWN SPEED/LEVEL OFF

GROSS WEIGHT 1000 KG		OPTIMUM DRIFT DOWN SPEED KIAS	LEVEL OFF ALTITUDE 1000 FT		
START DRIFT DOWN	LEVEL OFF		ISA + 10°C & BELOW	ISA + 15°C	ISA + 20°C
400	391 (385)	305 (296)	27 (15)	26 (13)	25 (11)
380	372 (366)	299 (289)	29 (16)	28 (15)	26 (13)
360	352 (347)	290 (282)	30 (18)	29 (17)	28 (15)
340	333 (329)	283 (275)	32 (20)	31 (19)	29 (17)
320	314 (310)	276 (267)	33 (22)	32 (21)	31 (19)
300	294 (290)	266 (259)	34 (24)	34 (22)	33 (21)
280	275 (271)	259 (251)	36 (25)	35 (24)	34 (23)
260	255 (251)	249 (242)	37 (27)	37 (26)	36 (25)
240	235 (232)	240 (233)	39 (29)	38 (28)	38 (27)
220	215 (213)	228 (223)	40 (31)	40 (30)	39 (29)
200	196 (194)	217 (213)	42 (34)	42 (33)	41 (32)

AUTOBRAKE LANDING DISTANCES (M)

CONDITIONS
1) 2000FT PRES ALT & BELOW
2) TEMP ISA + 10°C & BELOW
3) NO TAIL WIND
4) DRY RUNWAY
5) TOUCHDOWN ASSUMED 500M PAST THRESHOLD

APPROACH SPEED KIAS	LANDING DISTANCES (M)				
	AUTOBRAKE SETTING				
	1	2	3	4	MAX
200	5120	4200	3610	3000	2320
190	4720	3910	3360	2800	2220
180	4250	3610	3080	2650	2050
170	3850	3230	2820	2350	1900
160	3450	2910	2550	2150	1750
150	3100	2620	2300	1930	1600
140	2770	2350	2080	1750	1480
130	2460	2110	1860	1570	1350
120	2170	1880	1670	1430	1260

NOTES:
1) FOR CONDITIONS OUTSIDE ABOVE REFER SUPPLEMENTARY NORMAL PROCEDURES

gation of the aircraft is controlled by triple inertial reference systems (IRS) using ring laser gyros for control. The triple IRS feeds the known mean position into the FMS and, should one IRS fail or give incorrect signals, it is outvoted by the other two systems.

At nearly six hours into the flight, we are crossing the Iranian border, still at FL330 and a message on the flight plan reminds the crew to call Karachi on 127.3 10min prior to reaching Danib. We reach Danib at 18.29, exactly on schedule. We then are instructed to call Karachi on the HF 3467. Use of HF is fairly common for *en route* navigation across Pakistan, India and remote parts of Australia. Although the equipment is old, its range is better than the VHF line of site transmissions. Listening to the HF radio is an interesting experience. The distant voices sound as if they are transmitting down a long tin tunnel. Because the land lines are sometimes unreliable, much of the handover from one station to the next is done using the HF, rather than telephone lines, increasing considerably the voice traffic on the airwaves.

As we approach Karachi, we can call for local information on 118.8 and 127.3, talking to Karachi radar on 123.7 and we pass overhead at 19.17. At Vasla, we call Ahmadabad approach on 119.7 for relay to Bombay and are exactly on our flight planned time of 7hr 25min from take-off. At Nagpur we call Calcutta Radio on HF 3470 as we continue on in the darkness over the Indian sub-continent.

The Boeing 747-400 is operated by a pair of independent flight management computers (FMC), the controls for which are on either side of the central control console between the pilots. In addition, there is also a standby navigation computer. On the left hand computer, by the captain, is displayed the progress page which gives the time past the last waypoint, and the estimated time of arrival (ETA) at the next waypoint, with the one beyond. It maintains the predicted fuel levels, with the expected fuel on board at landing. The ETA Singapore is displayed with the total distance to go. It drives the aircraft at its most economic speed and gives the time and distance to the next climb point. In our case, we maintain 33,000ft for the remainder of the route until the top of descent point.

The right hand FMC display contains up to 30 pages of information, including the legs page which gives a description of the way points and navigation information. Included in these pages

are the horizontal and vertical navigation, speeds and highest levels. In effect, these displays give all the detailed information, to which the crew may need to refer if there are any problems with the routine navigation systems.

Between the two FMC displays is the group of four thrust levers, the speed brake control on the left, the flaps controls on the right and the fuel control switches — previously known as high pressure cocks — just behind the thrust levers. The trim controls — which used to be on the control console — are now located as switches on the control column. The trimming of the aircraft keeps it in neutral balance during the cruise by the use of miniature controls on the main control surfaces, and avoids undue control column loads.

Behind the thrust levers are the main communications and navigation equipment, including triple VHF radios, dual HF radios, two ADF (Automatic Direction Finders), two VOR (VHF Omnidirectional Radio Range) two DME (distance measuring equipment) and triple ILS (instrument landing systems). The ADF give bearings to the next beacon and the DME gives the distance to run to the beacon, provided the equipment is tuned into the frequency which identifies it to the aircraft. The ILS is the basis of the autoland system, which is cleared on the Boeing 747-400 to Cat IIIB — a decision height of nil and no forward visibility. The limitation on landing in these conditions is the visibility for taxying off the runway, which can be assisted to some extent by ground radar. However, the height of the Boeing 747-400 flightdeck from the ground makes any visual reference difficult in really thick fog. Autoland is only used when really required, as the pilots prefer to make manual landings to maintain recency. To achieve recency, the captain needs to make a manual landing at least once every 28 days, while the first officer has to fly in the aircraft at least once in every 28 days as operating crew. The first officer needs to make manual landings at least three times in a three-month period and operating as part of the heavy crew does not give any qualification towards recency. If a member of the crew becomes out of date, prior to a trip, he will spend a sortie on the full flight simulator, which provides a realistic operating environment. So close is the simulator to real operating conditions that all emergency training is undertaken on this equipment which saves any hazard to the actual aircraft. In fact some emergencies can be tested on the simulator, which could never be contemplated on the real aircraft.

Also located on the central console is ACARS (Aircraft Communications and Reporting System), which provides a direct data link to the ground of the performance of the aircraft systems. Close by are the passenger signs for no smoking and fasten seat belts, which are either switched on, off, or automatic, and the rudder trim indicator. A transponder is fitted; this is also known as secondary surveillance radar. This equipment, when set to a four-figure identity specified by air traffic control, puts that number on the blip on the radar screen, making the aircraft instantly recognisable to the controller in a crowded sky. Before transponders, an aircraft was required to make a specified turn, to identify it to the controller on the radar. If an aircraft is not flying in controlled airspace, it is normal to use the conspicuity code of 7000, if there is an emergency 7700 and 7600 informs of a radio failure. These later two figures automatically alert the ATC both orally and visually of the aircraft's problem before any other communications are made.

Finally, on the central console, is the automatic brake selector. This is particularly useful in an aborted take-off, where it sets the appropriate rate of deceleration better than it can be achieved manually. Care of the brakes is essential to keep the wheels as cool as possible and reverse thrust of the engines is used on every landing to save undue wear and tear on the brakes, even through it uses more fuel.

Above and between the two pilots is the roof panel with a further range of systems controls. At the rear are the least important items covering maintenance and circuit breakers. The latter isolates a faulty electrical system, much like a fuse in a domestic property. In the middle part of the panel is an area which one hopes is rarely, if ever, used. This is the fire control panel for the engines and auxiliary power unit. In the unlikely event of an engine fire, the fuel is cut off, the engine stopped and automatic fire extinguishers kill the fire. The fire, or overheating, is detected by firewires located all around the engine, a break or overheating being rapidly detected and signalled to the flightdeck to avoid undue damage to the engine.

More frequently used in the roof panel are the engine starting controls, which, when selected to auto start, drive an air-driven starter motor on each engine and, with the automatic switching-on of the fuel, starts the engines. As we saw on BA 011, two engines can be started at once to save time on the push back. The air pressure for the starter motor turbine is usually provided by bleed air from the APU, although this can also be supplied from a ground starter trolley if the aircraft remains static.

In the forward centre part of the roof panel are located the controls for the fuel system, allowing the movement of fuel from different zones to keep the aircraft in balance, as well as the airframe and automatic engine de-icing panel.

On the captain's side of the upper panel are the electrical engine controls (EEC) giving the minimum and maximum power electronically. The fly by wire (FBW) control is through the EEC sensing the speed, temperature and pressures. This helps to avoid any engine damage in advance. The captain has access to the electrical and hydraulic system controls and the panel for the three inertial reference systems (IRS) is located close by in the roof panel. The first officer has access on the right-hand side to the environmental control system (ECS) and the aircraft lights, both internal and external. When an aircraft is being operated, in the air or on the ground, it normally has a red light at the port wing-tip, a green on the starboard wing-tip and a white light in the tail. As an additional visual aid, it is normal to have rotating red beacons under the fuselage and either on the tail or on the top of the fuselage. Additionally strobe lights are often mounted on the wing-tips as a further means of attracting attention. Landing lights are used on most approaches to land in order to increase the visual conspicuousness of the aircraft for the controllers in the tower, whether by day or night. Lights are directed to shine along the wing leading edge to help detect icing conditions at night, and many airlines highlight their image by having 'logo' lights mounted in the tail plane to illuminate their tail markings in the dark.

After 10hr in the air and with about two hours to go, the heavy crew of Arthur Johnson and Philip Morley begin the preparation for arrival as dawn breaks — welcoming a new day for BA 011 —although it is still 22.30 back in Britain. We are in communication with Madras Flight Information Region (FIR) on HF 3470 as we pass over Port Blair in the Indian Ocean *en route* for Phuket. Since leaving the Indian coastline at Merok, we have been on airway B579, which takes us well south of Bangkok and thereby we avoid over flying Burma. We contact Singapore for a weather check and at 21.00 have reported wind of 350°, 4kt visibility of 10nm in rain and QNH pressure setting of 1,012mb. The weather at Kuala Lumpur is wind calm, visibility 4 km in mist and QNH of 1,013 and with no significant change expected. At 22.00, there is no change at either airfield, and a further check

Right:
Singapore approach chart for Runway 02R.

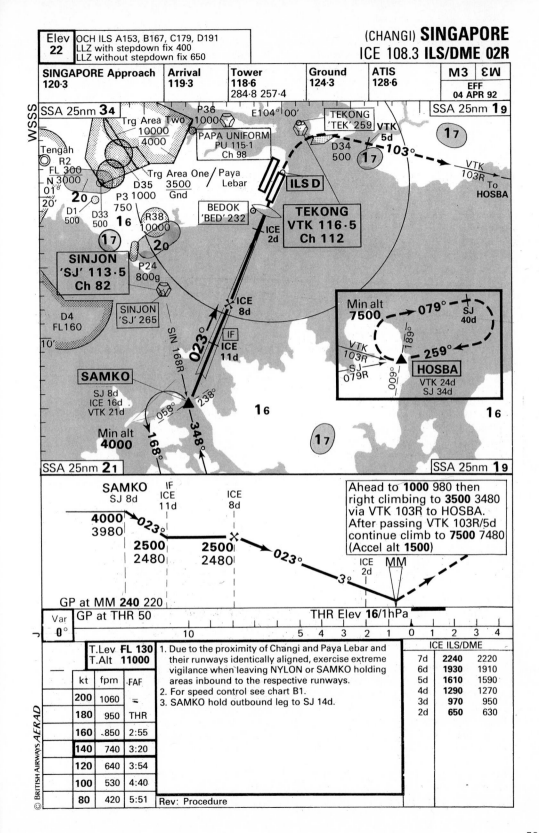

| Elev 22 | OCH ILS A153, B167, C179, D191 LLZ with stepdown fix 400 LLZ without stepdown fix 650 | | | | (CHANGI) **SINGAPORE** ICE 108.3 **ILS/DME 02R** | |

SINGAPORE Approach 120·3	Arrival 119·3	Tower 118·6 284·8 257·4	Ground 124·3	ATIS 128·6	M3	EW
					EFF 04 APR 92	

Ahead to **1000** 980 then right climbing to **3500** 3480 via VTK 103R to HOSBA. After passing VTK 103R/5d continue climb to **7500** 7480 (Accel alt **1500**)

GP at MM **240** 220
GP at THR 50
THR Elev **16**/1hPa

Var **0°**

	ICE ILS/DME	
7d	**2240**	2220
6d	**1930**	1910
5d	**1610**	1590
4d	**1290**	1270
3d	**970**	950
2d	**650**	630

T.Lev **FL 130** T.Alt **11000**		1. Due to the proximity of Changi and Paya Lebar and their runways identically aligned, exercise extreme vigilance when leaving NYLON or SAMKO holding areas inbound to the respective runways. 2. For speed control see chart B1. 3. SAMKO hold outbound leg to SJ 14d.
kt	fpm	.FAF
200	1060	≡
180	950	THR
160	.850	2:55
140	740	3:20
120	640	3:54
100	530	4:40
80	420	5:51

Rev: Procedure

© BRITISH AIRWAYS AERAD

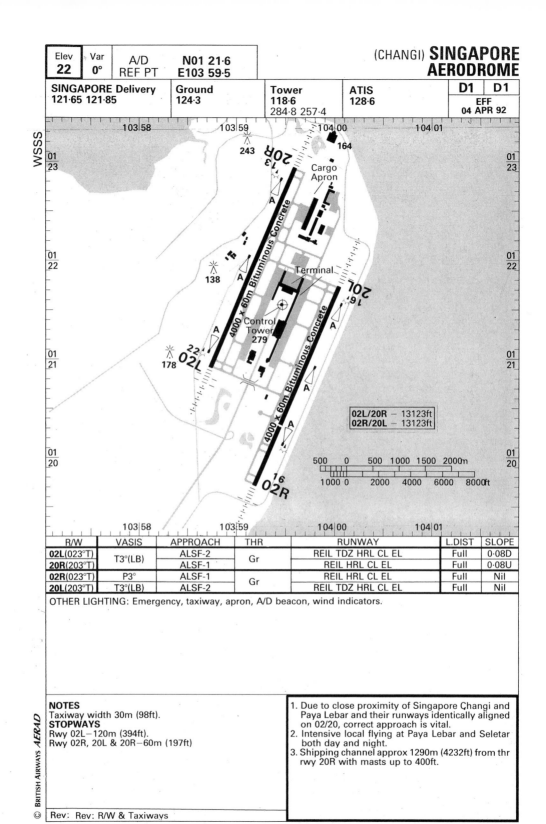

| | | | Elev 22 | Var 0° | A/D REF PT | N01 21·6 E103 59·5 | | | (CHANGI) **SINGAPORE AERODROME** |

| **SINGAPORE Delivery** 121·65 121·85 | **Ground** 124·3 | **Tower** 118·6 284·8 257·4 | **ATIS** 128·6 | **D1** | **D1** EFF **04 APR 92** |

WSSS

Cargo Apron

Terminal

Control Tower 279

4000 x 60m Bituminous Concrete

4000 x 60m Bituminous Concrete

| 02L/20R — 13123ft |
| 02R/20L — 13123ft |

500 0 500 1000 1500 2000m
1000 0 2000 4000 6000 8000ft

R/W	VASIS	APPROACH	THR	RUNWAY	L.DIST	SLOPE
02L(023°T)	T3°(LB)	ALSF-2	Gr	REIL TDZ HRL CL EL	Full	0·08D
20R(203°T)		ALSF-1		REIL HRL CL EL	Full	0·08U
02R(023°T)	P3°	ALSF-1	Gr	REIL HRL CL EL	Full	Nil
20L(203°T)	T3°(LB)	ALSF-2		REIL TDZ HRL CL EL	Full	Nil

OTHER LIGHTING: Emergency, taxiway, apron, A/D beacon, wind indicators.

NOTES
Taxiway width 30m (98ft).
STOPWAYS
Rwy 02L—120m (394ft).
Rwy 02R, 20L & 20R—60m (197ft)

1. Due to close proximity of Singapore Changi and Paya Lebar and their runways identically aligned on 02/20, correct approach is vital.
2. Intensive local flying at Paya Lebar and Seletar both day and night.
3. Shipping channel approx 1290m (4232ft) from thr rwy 20R with masts up to 400ft.

Rev: Rev: R/W & Taxiways

at 23.00 reveals the same situation with further mist forecast for Kuala Lumpur. There is, therefore, no reason why we should not continue to our planned destination of Singapore. The QNH pressure setting is altitude above sea level, whereas QFE is height above the airfield.

Ninety-one miles out from Phuket, at Tatox, we call Bangkok FIR on 120.5, changing to Bangkok Radio on 123.95, while maintaining contact on HF3470 with Rangoon and Lumpur Control. We make our landfall at Phuket on the coast of Thailand and, after nearly 11hr flying, we are around nine minutes behind time, but expect to land on schedule.

It is now time for Paul and Nigel to return as operating crew to control the descent and landing. We fly down airway R325 over Penang to Alor Setar just north of Kula Lumpur before joining airway A464 on the final run down the Malaysian coastline towards Singapore.

Having settled into their seats for the final hour, while still at FL330, the crew begin their descent briefing. We will be under radar control for landing on runway 02L and a QDM gives a magnetic bearing of 023 for the runway approach. The descent briefing covers our safety altitude and the transition level of 130. We check any unserviceabilities, of which there are none, and the weather conditions at our destination, which are reported as offering nothing significant. The first officer flies the aircraft from top of descent on the approach to 1,000ft altitude, when the captain will take over for landing. The IRS is fully serviceable and we will fly a standard arrival (STAR). The runway state is dry and we will use reverse thrust and autobraking as standard. The approach details are to use SAMKO as the final reporting point, which is 14 miles from the runway threshold, our safety altitude is between 1,700 and 2,000ft and we will make our final approach down the ILS. In the event of a go around for any reason, the decision height is 220ft, the flap setting being 20° with a positive climb on the flight director to 1,100ft. The undercarriage will be raised and a further climb made to 3,000ft with flaps raised to 5° and the climb speed to be 10kt above the minimum speed. The descent/approach checks are then made covering: Recall — checked; Briefing — confirmed; VREF — set; Minima — Set; and, altimeters QNH cross-checked after transition level.

We dial up 123.25 on the VHF and call 'Singapore Speedbird one one' and are changed to Singapore radar on 133.25. We are identified as reaching VBA at 15 level 330 MC25, runway 02 and maintain 330. VBA is just north of Kuala Lumpur. At the top of descent our IAS is 276 Mach 0.77 and our ground speed is 448kt.

Nigel confirms he has control, which is acknowledged by Paul to avoid any misunderstanding.

'Singapore Speedbird one one request descent.'

'Speedbird one one descend to level 270 heading 120°.'

At this point a warning — 'Bleed 1' shows in yellow on the engine display — and it is turned off. This means that reverse thrust may not be available on that engine, so care will be taken on landing. The fault is entered in the technical report and a computer printout code gives the complete maintenance instruction to rectify the fault.

'Descend ten thousand QNH 1013.'

'Cleared direct JB Speedbird one one.'

'IAS 320 in descent, heading 112.'

'Speedbird one one change to 120.3.'

'Singapore approach Speedbird one one passing 173.'

'Speedbird one one descend to 6000 02R, no speed restriction.'

We are 15min to touch down, flying over the offshore islands to the south of Malaysia and tracking over the western side of the island of Singapore to the south, turning to line up with runway 02 right.

'Speedbird one one turn right heading 155.'

We lower flap 1 which is the wing leading-edge only. We set VHF 119.3 and at 6,000ft are No 2 in sequence to land on runway 02R. Flaps 5 are selected, speed 200 depending on our weight and the power levers follow. Our heading is 156 as we pass through the extended centre line of the runway. 'Cabin ready' is checked to ensure passengers are strapped in, seats are upright, no smoking signs are on and the cabin attendants are seated.

'Speedbird one one descend to 4,000ft.'

'Speedbird one one ready to turn.'

'Roger.'

'Speedbird one one left 350.'

'Turn left 350 Speedbird one one.'

'Speedbird one one descend 2,500ft.'

'Speedbird one one heading 330.'

'One one 17 miles from touch down.'

At 4,000ft, the autopilot is disconnected, Nigel is flying by hand.

'Speedbird one one turn right 350°, cleared ILS 02R.'

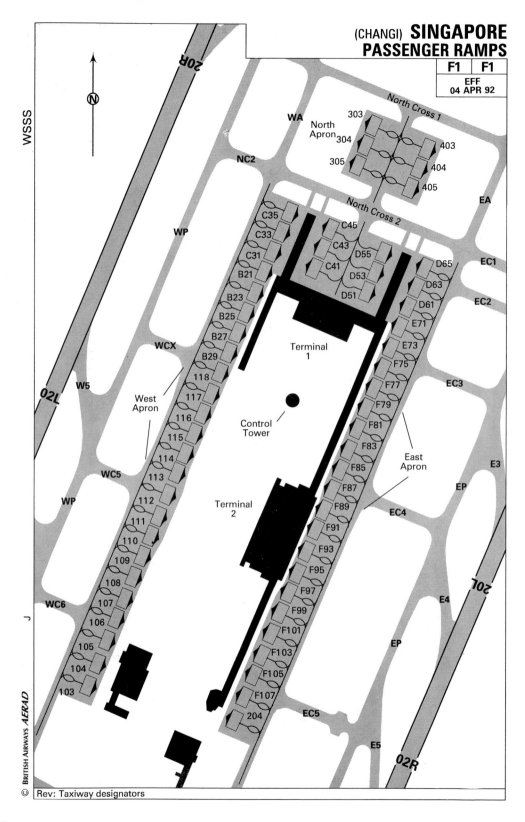

(CHANGI) **SINGAPORE PASSENGER RAMPS**

F1	F1

EFF
04 APR 92

Rev: Taxiway designators

© BRITISH AIRWAYS *AERAD*

Above:
BA Boeing 747-400 G-BNLW after arrival at stand E71 at Singapore.

Left:
The Singapore Passenger Ramps Chart shows stand E71 between taxiways EC2 and EC3.

'Speedbird one one established 02R, change to Singapore Tower on 118.6.'

Gear down and flaps 20. We have the airfield in sight in sunshine. The landing check list is called: Speedbrake — armed; autobrake — set; landing gear — down; flaps — 20 green; cabin crew — report received. Landing checks complete.

Singapore tower: 'Speedbird one one, clear land 350°, 9kt.'

'Clear land, Speedbird one one.'

Paul takes control at 1,000ft.

The speed brake is selected and flaps lowered to 25°, over the airport boundary, Nigel calling the heights above the runway: 100, 50, 30, landing at 12.55 or 08.55 local — reverse. There is no problem with the reverse thrust in the number one engine and, as we begin to slow to taxi speed, we change to ground on 124.3 clearing the runway to the left on EC3 towards stand E71 on the nearest side of the terminal building at Singapore. The weather radar is turned off and the APU is started in preparation for providing ground power.

Nigel runs through the after landing check list, while Paul continues to taxi to our allocated stand. Strobes — off; stabiliser — six units; speedbrake — down; flaps — up; APU electrics — available. As we approach stand, we call the cabin crew to switch doors to manual.

We still have 24.7 tonnes of fuel left as we come to a stop, nose in on the red light and the air bridge commences to move out towards the cabin door just behind the first-class cabin. Brakes are on, switches off and chocks are under the wheels at 09.00 local time. With the usual activity of the passengers scrambling for their carry-on baggage in the cabin, we run through the shutdown checklist on the flightdeck covering: hydraulic demand pumps — off; fuel pump switches — off; aft cargo heat (the dog) — off; weather radar — off; park brake — as required; fuel control switches — cut off.

As the crew prepare to leave the aircraft and the passengers depart, we join the people in transit to wander through the massive Changi airport terminal. At the same time the aircraft is cleaned, the Singapore luggage and cargo is removed, the refuelling commences and the old catering is switched for the new. As well as the flightdeck crews, the cabin crew also depart the aircraft at Changi for a rest, a complete new crew taking over the Boeing 747-400 for the flight to Sydney, and more for the final destination of Melbourne.

4. The Cabin Crew

The perceived image of the cabin crew on duty aboard passenger aircraft is generally of people who serve food and drink to keep the occupants quiet between the movies on the long-haul flights. However, the prime purpose of their presence on board is to ensure the safety, security and well-being of the passengers. The food and drink is an important secondary task as part of the customer service duties. The cabin crew work long hours aboard the average long-haul fight, often at times when most of us prefer to be trying to sleep. They must stay smart, alert and attentive throughout their long duty period.

After a rigourous initial selection process, they are trained in all the safety aspects, and have to undertake regular annual training to demonstrate they are still current on the emergency procedures. In the unlikely event of an emergency evacuation, the departure of the passengers is achieved far quicker under the control of the cabin crew, who, as a result, are the last to leave the aircraft. The cabin crew need to pass an annual half-day medical and they are also trained to cover a range of medical emergencies, more than the average first aid, using onboard medical and drug kits. Some of them also have some professional medical or nursing experience but, in time of real need, it can almost certainly be guaranteed that there will be a doctor on board. Such a person would be identified from the passenger list rather than a request across the public address system, which can guarantee to alarm some of the more nervous passengers. The cabin crew are responsible for the general welfare of the passengers, including unaccompanied children, elderly people — particularly those who are first-time flyers, providing information, concern and compassion. On our flight to Singapore was a honeymoon couple who were presented with a greetings card signed by the crew and a bottle of champagne, and a youngster celebrating a birthday had a cake presented — all part of the customer service. In addition, as part of the marketing operation of British Airways, the cabin staff offer duty free goods for those passengers who were short of time at the airport, or for the last minute good quality gift or souvenir.

The cabin crew on each flight are not a regular team and, with some 10,000 cabin staff employed overall by British Airways, it is fairly rare to meet someone known. On some festive flights, such as at Christmas and the New Year, crews can request to travel with particular colleagues so that they at least have the opportunity to share the celebration with someone they know.

In overall charge of the cabin crew is the Cabin Service Director and, on our flight, this is Gwylym Hitchcock. Gwylym will have celebrated flying on the line for 26 years in February 1993. He very much enjoys his work with the contact with people and the travel, and prefers it to a home-based job of 'flying a desk'. Gwylym started his career with BOAC, later flying on the long-haul fleet of VC-10s or Boeing 707s for about eight and a half years. He then moved on to the early Boeing 747s and has worked on Jumbo jets ever since, his licence covering all the versions in service with British Airways.

The Cabin Service Director is provided with a cabin service inflight information sheet, identifying the flight number, departure date and time, aircraft type, registration and seating configuration. The configuration of our Boeing 747-400 is for 18 First Class, 74 Club World and 293 World Traveller passengers. There is a full list of the cabin crew names identifying their seniority and division. Two of the cabin crew are Singapore-based. The scheduled times of departure and arrival at the various *en route* stops and destination are noted at local times with the GMT variation. The expected passenger compliment is noted, but there is always a number of no shows, so the catering is adjusted for the anticipated load. The requirement for special meals is noted, but none are requested for BA 011. There is also a list of passenger special requirement, including two meet and assist, one medical, 10 VIPs and two wheelchair patients. Smoking rows on this flight are noted at No 4 in First Class, Nos 22 and 23 in Club World and Nos 48-53 in World Traveller. There is also a list of the video movies being screened; the duration of our flight allows time for four complete films.

On our flight today from London to Singapore, we have 12 First Class passengers, 41 Club World and 178 World Travellers. On the 747-400 the upper-deck is configured for World Travellers, as is the rear half of the main deck behind Club World. The cabin crew are rostered 28 days in advance by computer. The computer matches the cost effectiveness of time and logs the destinations over the previous 30 trips to give a fair coverage to all cabin crew members. Crew members can, of course, request a particular trip and will usually achieve it but, if there is a conflict, seniority will decide. Each Cabin Service Director manages three or four pursers, and they tend to form the only regular part of the cabin crew team.

The cabin crew are expected to check-in at the British Airways staff car park 1hr 25min before departure where they are briefed by the Cabin Services Director, who usually checks in 2hr 25min before departure to give him time to gather the information to prepare for the briefing. The cabin crew sign the crew record sheet to confirm they are fit to fly, rested and have all the necessary documents. In his briefing, the Cabin Services Director allocates members of the team to their cabin work areas, establishes who has any additional language skills, and passes out all the technical data. He advises on the nature of the load, any special passengers or special diets and Executive Club gold card carriers. To keep the staff commercially aware, the overall cost of fare or value volume is given. A random safety check is made.

One hour 10min prior to departure, the cabin crew leave the reporting centre on BA crew buses through the regular security checks to the aircraft on its stand. Once aboard they complete their final preparations prior to the passengers' loading time, 45min before departure.

Before departure, the evacuation alarm and public address systems are checked as serviceable, as both are essential in any emergencies. Should an emergency evacuation be required a total evacuation has to be achieved within 90sec, considerably quicker than the normal departure of the passengers on arrival at the destination.

Each cabin has a purser who manages the customer service in his or her area. Ian Sturgess is the purser in Club World, and each purser bids for his task according to seniority. The duties of the purser are to ensure that the customers receive the British Airways' product to the highest standard. The purser gives low key supervision to the cabin crew, ensuring that the presentation and delivery is up to the customers' expectation. The basis for the entire operation is team work, including being totally flexible and helping out other crew members as required. Every member of the cabin crew has to pass the CAA safety tests and each one is allocated a particular emergency exit in the event of a need.

The Cabin Service Director, Gwilym Hitchcock, catches up with some of the paperwork in his small office during a lull in the passenger service duties.

The Cabin Services Director is provided with a five-page briefing document, together with a list of all the passengers on board. We have two elderly passengers on this flight, with their seat allocation identified, as they will need assistance in boarding and disembarking. There is an asthmatic passenger who must be located in a no-smoking area. There is also a list of any passengers who might be considered VIPs, and the total list of passengers gives a range of information to the cabin crew, such as names, addresses, profession and any special interests. Much of this data is gained from membership of the BA Executive Club and allows the cabin crew to be able to converse with regular fliers on subjects which particularly interest them. This feature is part of the BA policy of customer care to make regular travellers comfortable and to avoid their feeling just part of the travelling masses.

The briefing sheet covers a few typical safety questions and answers which can be tried out on the cabin crew to ensure that they are up to date with the workings of the aircraft. There are also some current notices, keeping the cabin crew up to date with the latest news of BA activities, such as new competitions for the passengers on various routes.

The text of the passenger announcements is supplied covering the arrival at each of the destinations, one of the restrictions being that Australian Government regulations prohibit smoking on all aircraft whilst flying between Australian cities. This will affect the final leg between Sydney and Melbourne. There is the usual information about partner hotels and car rentals, Executive Club members possibly benefiting from discounts and upgrades. There are instructions covering arrival in Sydney for passengers who are either making an international or domestic connection, as well as providing information on the bus services into the City of Sydney. A warning is given that passengers should make sure they keep sufficient funds for the Aus $20.00 departure tax for every passenger, which supposedly was in currency only, but in practice credit cards were also acceptable. British nationals travelling to Australia need a visa and must also complete a landing card.

Australian regulations require that all international flights are sprayed internally with an

approved anti-bug spray before the doors are closed at the last port of call, and at the top of descent before landing. This conforms with the Australian Agriculture and Health requirements, the non-toxic spray approved by the World Health Organisation avoids the introduction of harmful insects into Australia. Due to the Quarantine Regulations all food must be left on board or placed in quarantine bins. During transit stops, passengers may remain on board but, if they wish, they may take some exercise in the transit lounge.

During the long flight from London to Singapore, the cabin crew are on duty for over 12hr in addition to their check-in and finishing times. This obviously makes a very long day, as there are no 'heavy crew' substitutes in the cabin. Therefore, during the quieter periods, between meals and when the movies are running, members of the cabin crew can take rest periods in a special rest area in the rear of the aircraft above the toilets. There is room for up to eight people to have a break on bunks, to refresh themselves for later on in the flight when the cabin becomes busy again. Each member of the cabin crew has a minimum of three hours rest, lying horizontal.

The cabin crew will have two nights rest in Singapore before picking up duty on a Singapore-Perth flight, after which they will have a further night stop. They then return to Singapore for two nights rest before heading back to London. There will then be five nights rest at home before being rostered on to their next trip.

In addition to the duty cabin crew, as already mentioned we have two Fleet Directors on board, who have their own management tasks independent of the duty crew. Keith Owen is responsible for managing up to 150 cabin crew and his duties require him to fly on the routes about once every three weeks to keep him in touch with his team. Rather than being rostered away most of the year, Keith probably spends just over half the year out of the office and is self-rostering according to the needs of the job. He is one of about 30 Fleet Directors allocated to the long-haul, wide-bodied Boeing 747 fleet. This group manages some 4,000 cabin crew.

Colin Sheath, the other Fleet Director, has duties, however, more typical of marketing. On our flight to Singapore, Colin was looking at the First Class product, particularly the catering service. It is difficult to compare meals on board the average flight with a top grade restaurant but, within the limitations, British Airways attain a high quality of service, covering both food and presentation. There are continuing efforts to enhance the standards, and evolve the product by trying new procedures, communicating with the staff and passengers to assess the results. The First Class passengers have their

Above:
Gisela Tan serves breakfast rolls in Club World.

Below:
Helen McGill serves breakfast coffee before arrival at Singapore.

own armrest video systems with individual selection of up to 55 different films, and featuring their own controls for adjustment. Skyphones and fax machines are already a reality in some regions of the world, due to the capability of the Satcom (Satellite Communications) systems now available. Some people would rather use a long flight to relax or work away from the distraction of the telephone, but the good news is that, for security reasons, only outgoing calls or faxes can be transmitted. There can probably be nothing more frustrating to passengers than to have one of their number constantly chattering on the telephone. As part of its customer service, British Airways is looking at integrating the total package of the journey, from departure from home or office to arrival at the destination hotel. Colin flies about once a month to assess practically the project in hand, as the airline is constantly looking for new products or improvements to stay ahead of the competition. Although First Class was the product on this occasion, British Airways is obviously looking at the overall product in all areas of the aircraft, particularly in these days of economic belt tightening, when business passengers are having to downgrade to conserve travel budgets. Good service will ensure that these people upgrade in better times on British Airways, instead of losing them to other carriers.

During our transit stop at Singapore, where some passengers departed, and a few more boarded for Australia, we took advantage of the opportunity to look around the modern terminal building at Changi. It is laid out in the shape of a large 'H' with aircraft gates right down both outer edges, and in one end of the terminal area. It is a very clean and efficient building, with shops and restaurants located in the central block. Singapore is very much a hub, as it is a major crossroads for international aviation travel with passengers journeying to and fro across Asia. The Pacific rim represents the world's fastest growing aviation travel market. Airliners from China, USA, Africa, Europe and Australia can be parked along each other, and Changi is also the home base for Singapore Airlines. Singapore Airlines is one of the most aggressive operators in the region, maintaining a very young fleet of modern jet airliners. Passengers in transit are dealt with very efficiently by the computer systems at the airport, with the friendly and communicative staff keeping close track of people and their baggage. It is probably one of the most user friendly airports in the world and, therefore, a delight to travel through, despite often the hustle and bustle of the airport at busy periods.

The new passengers are boarding and the more adventurous transit passengers return to the aircraft through the mandatory security system. We return to the flightdeck, where the new crew is expecting us. This has happened throughout the entire trip — a tribute to the organisation of the BA Public Relations department. Since Singapore-Sydney sector represents a relatively short flight duration and as the aircraft flies on to Melbourne with another crew, we only have the two operating crew. The pair is headed by Capt Richard Calcutt with senior first officer Dick Norriss. Richard and Dick have spent two nights in Singapore after bringing a flight out from London and will spend one night in Sydney before flying the return leg to Singapore. Some crews covering the more remote routes can be away from home for a week or more, before they bring a flight back to London.

On this leg of the flight we have 10 First Class passengers, 38 Club World and 285 World Travellers, plus 3,000kg of cargo in the underfloor hold, in addition to the normal baggage.

Our route takes us down the eastern side of the Indonesian islands of Sumatra and Java with Borneo on the left hand side. Our land fall in Australia is close to Derby on the northwest coast in Western Australia, and we fly right across the vast, arid deserts of the Northern Territory, between Queensland and South Australia, and across New South Wales to land at Sydney. Another crew will be at Sydney ready to take the aircraft on to Melbourne overnight.

The weather forecast is fairly typical of both the region and the season through which we will be flying. Upper winds at FL340 have components in our favour and the temperatures drop to minus 50°C over the latter part of the flight. The main weather to be encountered will be the forecasted thunderstorms down the entire length of Indonesia, which bring the possibility of clear air turbulence, followed by a clear area across the Indian Ocean and Australia, as far as

On the ground at Singapore, the Boeing 747-400 is prepared for departure. APU is running, the passenger doors are in manual and the park brake is set. Total fuel is 898,000kg. The hydraulic systems page is displayed on the lower screen.

Left:
Capt Richard Calcutt commences the pre-start checks.

Right:
Senior First Officer Dick Norriss prepares the navigation charts.

Left:
Capt Richard Calcutt runs through the emergency procedures.

Right:
The Boeing 747-400 cockpit roof panel.

Below:
Capt Calcutt enters data into the navigation system while Dick Norriss checks the weather map.

around Alice Springs, when more thunder-storms and clear air turbulence were expected. In the event, we were well above the cloud lay-ers during the early part of the flight and saw the build up of thunderclouds around NSW dur-ing our approach to Sydney. None of these caused any discomfort to our flight. Two inter-esting features on the weather map are typhoon 'Gay' centred east of the Philippines and a vol-canic ash cloud over the north coast of Papua New Guinea.

We tune into the Singapore ATIS and note Changi ATC Information E which gives: expect ILS approach runway 02, at 02.00 the VOR is unserviceable, wind 340 5kt, visibility 10km., cloud 1 octa 1,700ft, temperature 26°, dew point 24°, QNH 1,013, no significant change. For the take-off calculations, we will use runway 02R, the one we landed on, with flaps set at the take-off position of 20° from a dry runway. Our pres-sure altitude, being near to the coast, is 20. Our revised take off weight, corrected for .the

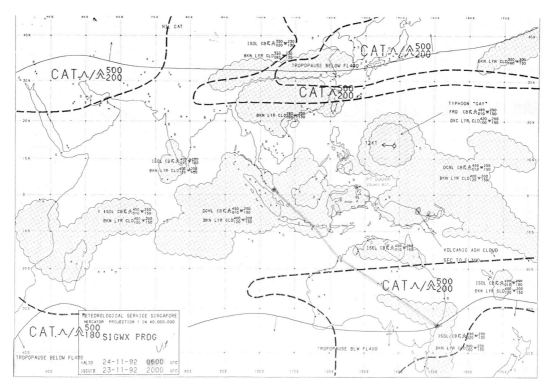

weather conditions is 437.9 tonnes and using an assumed temperature of 62°C, our wind component assumed take-off weight is 322.8 tonnes, somewhat less than our departure from Heathrow, but at a greater temperature, as would be expected. Our zero fuel weight is 234.3 tonnes and our landing weight was predicted at 252.6 tonnes.

The briefing summary for BA 011/23 Nov 92 runs to nearly 11 pages of print out, giving the crew an ETD of 02.25 GMT and confirming they can find their aircraft on Stand E71. There is less chance of confusion on the choice of aircraft at Singapore, as we are the only British Airways' aircraft parked amongst the fleet of Singapore Airlines.

The maintenance of the aircraft runways does not affect our flight as far as runway workings are concerned, because they are on specific days of the month which do not coincide with our visit. However, the east apron taxiway between bay 204 and the south across taxiway is closed 00.30 to 11.00 daily from 27 October to 9 February. Bays B25 and B27 and the taxiway behind are closed today, 24 November between 03.00 and 09.00. Our crew have to ensure they avoid these areas while taxying out for departure, although they expect to receive clear instructions from air traffic for the route to the runway threshold.

At Sydney, Kingsford Smith Airport, the wind is forecast as 290/5kt changing to 050/12kt all the nines, 3 octas cumulus 3,000ft with a 20% probability of occasional thunderstorms. The NOTAM (Notice to Airmen) information mainly refers to landings during the night time curfew which will not affect our flight. No landings are permitted at Sydney between 24.00 and 05.00 even as an alternate. By special dispensation landings may be allowed at Sydney from 23.00 to 24.00, and 05.00 to 06.00 local times on runway 34 which involves an approach over Botany Bay thereby reducing noise nuisance to the surrounding population. The reciprocal runway 16 is also available to take-offs, keeping the overflying aircraft from passing over the city of Sydney. When making landings during the curfew con- cession only reverse idle thrust should be used. If more reverse thrust is used due to operational requirements a report must be submitted to Canberra. The air-to-ground frequency of 130.9 is not available from 23 to 27 November, and this fact is noted. It was also noted that all parking stands at the international terminal had been renumbered. This could cause confusion to arriving aircraft without the new layout being issued from flight planning.

Our designated alternates for Sydney are Brisbane to the north and Melbourne to the south. Neither of these present any weather or operational problems in the event of a diversion, possibly caused by violent thunderstorms, from Sydney. Many of the navigation warnings and special briefings do not affect our proposed route, but we are warned to avoid the area of Mount Dukonoo due to volcanic activity at coordinate 0141 North 12752 East. The height of the dust was variable and, if flown through, it can have a sand-blasting effect on the airframe and engines. Other volcanic activity is noted, but is not close enough to our track to be of concern.

For information, a simulated operational trial is being undertaken in Australian airspace, but BA are not participating at this stage although

Left:
The weather chart for our flight from Singapore to Sydney, with thunderstorm activity forecast at both ends.

Below left:
Dick Norriss prepares for start up.

Below:
Push-back from stand E72 at Singapore.

Top:
We await the arrival of a Hercules before entering the runway.

Above:
BA Boeing 747-400 G-BNLW is about to roll from runway 02R whilst a Federal Express DC-10 taxies to the holding point.

Right:
Our departure chart from Singapore was a right turn-out after departure and down to Tanjung.

Trans alt **11000**		

1. Cruising levels will be issued after take-off by Singapore Control/Radar.
2. For min ROC gradients see chart B2.

G4	** t⅁**
EFF	
04 APR 92	

NOT TO SCALE

WSSS

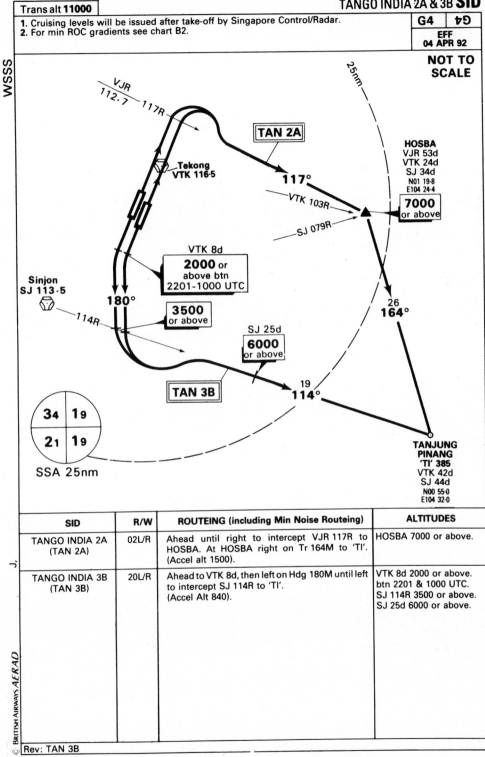

VJR 112.7 — 117R

TAN 2A

117°

VTK 103R

SJ 079R

Tekong VTK 116·5

HOSBA
VJR 53d
VTK 24d
SJ 34d
N01 19·8
E104 24·4
7000 or above

25nm

VTK 8d
2000 or above btn 2201-1000 UTC

Sinjon SJ 113·5

180°

114R

3500 or above

SJ 25d
6000 or above

26 **164°**

TAN 3B

19 **114°**

TANJUNG PINANG
'TI' 385
VTK 42d
SJ 44d
N00 55·0
E104 32·0

3₄	1₉
2₁	1₉

SSA 25nm

SID	R/W	ROUTEING (including Min Noise Routeing)	ALTITUDES
TANGO INDIA 2A (TAN 2A)	02L/R	Ahead until right to intercept VJR 117R to HOSBA. At HOSBA right on Tr 164M to 'TI'. (Accel alt 1500).	HOSBA 7000 or above.
TANGO INDIA 3B (TAN 3B)	20L/R	Ahead to VTK 8d, then left on Hdg 180M until left to intercept SJ 114R to 'TI'. (Accel Alt 840).	VTK 8d 2000 or above. btn 2201 & 1000 UTC. SJ 114R 3500 or above. SJ 25d 6000 or above.

Rev: TAN 3B

clarification was being sought from the Australian CAA. We were assured that it would not have any effect on the aircraft landing sequence or result in significant delays. We were alerted to the requirement to contact Perth international HF at least 20min prior to reaching the Australian FIR boundary, if we were above FL245 inbound to Australian Airspace, in our case on airway A576, until 17 December at 06.00. The crew are reminded that the Australian Quarantine clearance is a legal requirement and must be passed by radio on the company frequency for first point of entry into Australia. Various restricted areas are active at a number of times, but either the timing or position means they are of no concern to our flight.

Our dangerous and special loads as before cover the aerosol anti-insect canisters, which have to be supplied empty to the Australian authorities as proof of their use, and we still have the long-distance dog on board.

The weather at the *en route* alternates is given. The most obvious alternate is Jakarta Soekarno which was reporting rain, but forecasting an improvement in the cloud levels through the period. Runway 07L/25R at Jakarta was closed, but the parallel runway 07R/25L was fully available.

Our minimum cost flight plan gives us an initial cruising altitude of FL290, climbing to FL330 at Aktod and then to FL370 at Akula. Our total fuel is 89,843kg including contingency of 3,511kg, diversion allowance of 10,493kg and reserves of 4,299kg. For taxying to take-off 1,300kg is estimated as the allowance. Our flight planned distance is 3,454nm taking an elapsed time of 6hr 46min.

Our crew run through all the normal preparations and checks including the external walkround similar to those at Heathrow, but the weather is certainly more pleasant. The catering is loaded and stowed while the passengers board and are settled in. The captain runs through his briefing to ensure a complete understanding in case there is any form of emergency on departure, and all preparation and checks are complete at 02.17 GMT, 10.17 local, nearly two and a half hours after our arrival,. This gives some idea of the complex activity in turning round a modern jet airliner for its next journey.

The crew will receive their departure frequency with their clearance and the passenger access bridge is away at 02.21. Singapore tower calls 'Speedbird one one, you are cleared to flight level 370'. Our response is negative due to our heavy fuel load of 89.9 tonnes. 'Speedbird one one, flight level 270 available.' We request FL330, but there may be a delay of more than half an hour before there is room at this level, due to a pair of overflights of Singapore already established on our designated airway A576. We, therefore, accept FL270 to save the delay, even though it will be more costly, in the hope we will be able to achieve a better altitude as our fuel load decreases. We are asked to squawk 2243 on our transponder.

For a while the higher overflying traffic is going to cause a block to our flight gaining its desired altitude on the busy A576 all the way to Sydney. The aircraft concerned are at least one Boeing 767 which has a slightly lower cruising speed to the 747-400 and perhaps, if we can pass by underneath, we can obtain a clearance to increase our cruising altitude in front of this traffic if there is nothing else immediately ahead.

We call Singapore ground control on 124.3 giving our call sign and position on stand E71 request push-back and engine start for runway 02R, facing south on the taxiway. Ground control gives us clearance to push-back and, with the release of the brakes, autostart is selected first with engines Nos 4 and 3, followed by Nos 2 and 1. The aircraft beacons are switched on and the doors selected to automatic. We push back at 02.25 GMT and the engines are running.

'Speedbird one one clear taxi on EC3 and EP 02 right.' As we commence moving at 02.30 GMT our take-off checks are completed with controls full and free, flaps set at 20°, trim set and the transponder checked.

The crew are steering the aircraft from quite a considerable height above the ground and have to ensure adequate clearance all round. No-one wants to be the first to knock off the new extended wing tip of the 747-400. The yellow lines along the taxiways help keep the aircraft on centre and the crew are located almost directly above the steerable nose wheel. Not only do the wings need clearance, but as the nose turns, so the massive tail swings around behind, and the engines generate a fair amount of jet blast as can be imagined to propel this large aircraft into the air.

'Singapore Tower, Speedbird one one is taxiing to the holding point 02R and ready for departure.'

'Speedbird one one clear for departure after one touch and go traffic.' We look up the approach path and see a distant dot inbound with its tell-tail trail of black smoke. It is C-130 Hercules and we wonder why we cannot leave

Right:
Chart ASI/6 shows our route from Singapore on Airway A576 to Bali.

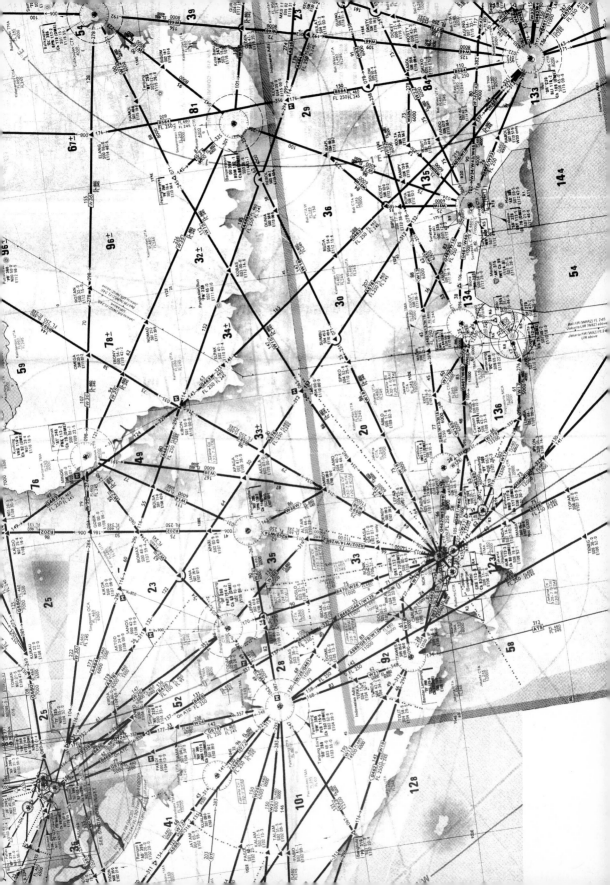

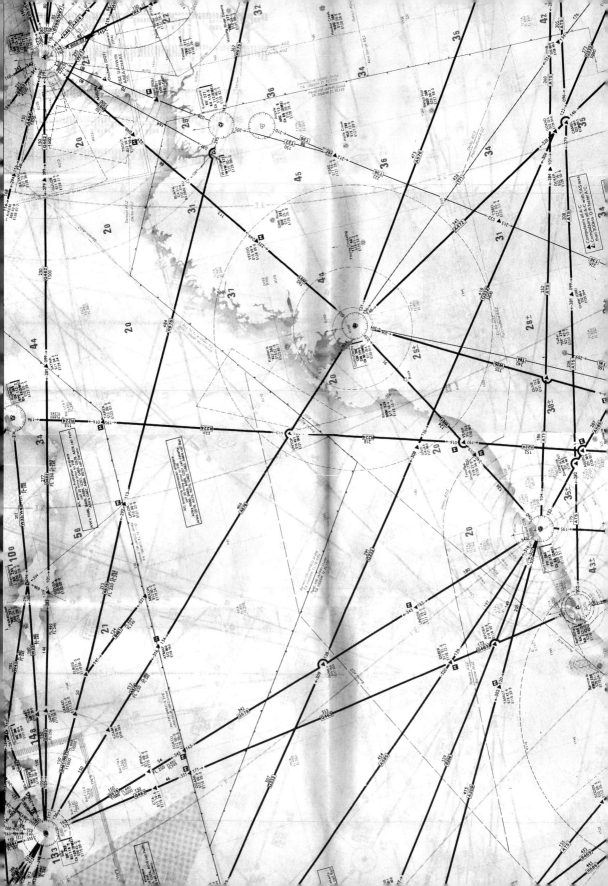

in front of it, as there is plenty of time, but we are held perhaps due to our jet wash. We are also surprised to see a group of workmen in the undershoot area close to the threshold as they do not seem concerned by the blast of our jet exhaust which they will shortly endure.

When the Hercules has passed, we hear the call 'Speedbird one one, line up on the runway and wait,' which we acknowledge 'Wind 350/10kt'.

'Speedbird one one, climb to 5,000, clear for take-off.' We acknowledge 'Singapore Tower, climb to 5,000, clear for take off, Speedbird one one'. The time is 02.42 GMT.

The power is set and we begin rolling along the runway with the Changi terminal on our left, our V_1 is 151kt, V_R 155kt and V_2 162kt as we rotate and climb away past the Singapore Airways maintenance base to our left below, the undercarriage is selected up on a heading of 023. 'Contact 120.3 Singapore approach.'

'Speedbird one one passing 1,000ft, climb to 8000 track 022.' The flaps begin to be retracted, first to 10°, and then to five degrees.

'Speedbird one one, turn right heading 120, flight level 150.'

'Turn right, heading 120, flight level 150, Speedbird one one.'

All clearances and instructions are repeated to avoid confusion, but information such as weather is noted. As we turn on to the new heading, speed check is called to ensure we keep well clear of the stalling speed as we continue our climb. Flaps one and flaps up are called and actioned, and the air conditioning controls are set.

'Speedbird one one own nav, clear TI.'

'TI one one heading 139.' TI is the VOR at Tandjung where we join airway A576 10min after take-off.

'Speedbird one one, call Singapore Radar 128.1.'

'Singapore radar 128.1, Speedbird one one.'

'Singapore radar, Speedbird one one out of 6500, flight level 150.'

'Climb to level 270, Speedbird one one, heading 140.' We are climbing at 2,800ft per minute and are due over Bali at 04.39 GMT, which is within one minute of our flight plan. Our total scheduled time is 7hr 30min, chock to chock, which includes ground manoeuvring at each end of the flight.

Mention was made in Chapter 3 of ACARS —

Left:
Chart AUS/1 shows our route across the sea to landfall in Australia at Derby and then we continue on the same airway toward Pavko.

Airborne Communications, Addressing and Reporting System. This is management by digital air/ground communications giving the airline operations department in real time the current status of the aircraft in both operational and engineering terms.

A modern airliner is a very expensive capital asset to buy and also costly to operate. However, when it is being operated, it, at least, has the potential of making a profit, whereas, when on the ground, it becomes a total loss maker. Airliners are often in the control of a variety of crews, operating for extended periods in parts of the world remote from their home base. The only company communications are generally with the local station managers on the company VHF frequency, which can only be used for the briefest of data so as not to clog up the valuable airwave time. With the sophistication of modern aircraft avionics, there are more efficient methods to download important data in real time.

An airline operations department task is to make sure the fleet is used to its maximum efficiency, ideally by tracking the individual aircraft and meeting their respective needs. Like many industries, aviation is served by its fair share of jargon and one of these is 'oooitimes' — the operations department identification of one of their prime needs 'out, off, on, in time'. This means aircraft times for chocks away, take-off, landing and on-chocks. Piedmont Airlines in the USA were the first airline in the world to achieve real time 'oooitimes' at their operation centre from 1977 through the use of ACARS. This is another piece of aviation jargon meaning an Arinc aeronautical digital communications system. By installing switches on various operational parts of the aircraft — such as the main entry door, parking brakes and main undercarriage — messages can be sent by data link to the home base keeping track of the aircraft movements. Although ACARS is gradually becoming worldwide on the major trunk routes covering North America, Europe, Middle East, Central and Southeast Asia and Australia, it is managed in the USA by Arinc, in Canada by Air Canada and by the Sita network in the rest of the world. These management systems are fully compatible and linked to each other to maintain the most complete cover, and this cover is continuing to expand.

The two major reasons for choosing an ACARS system is either for ops driven or engineering driven information, although the combination of both needs is most desirable for an overall improvement in management of the fleet. We have already covered briefly the engineering driven information in Chapter 3. The use of

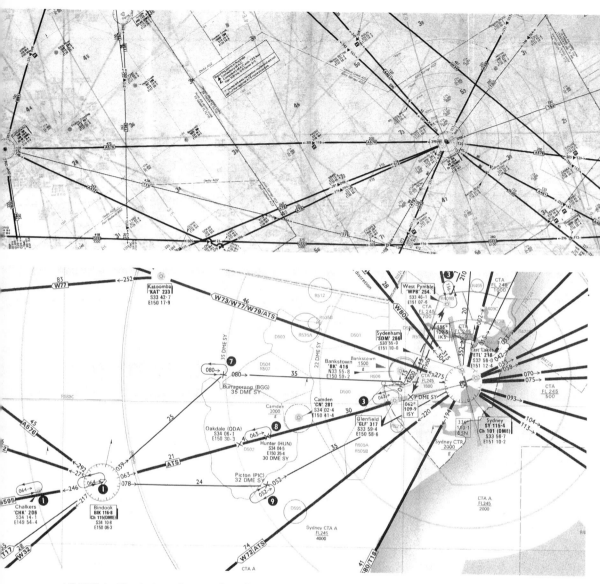

ACARS in North America was largely ops driven as the systems became established, but Europe and Australia could take advantage of being late in adopting the system to introduce a wider information service, with no initial limit on the boundaries. It has been the advent of the digital aircraft — such as the Airbus A320 and Boeing 747-400 — which inspired the introduction of the new communications system. These aircraft are already equipped with ACMS (aircraft conditioning monitoring systems), DAR (digital airworthiness recorders) and Bite (Built in test equipment) with a capacity for monitoring the systems health of the aircraft in real time. Any pilot-reported information may only be briefly transmitted during the flight, or after arrival at the destination, and any detailed technical data would have to be downloaded when convenient. The computers on modern aircraft can analyse much more information than the operating crew and transmit this data in a fraction of the time. Pilots can only report after the event has happened, rather than prevent it happening, which diagnostic computers can help to achieve.

Although the normal air traffic VHF frequency band is used by ACARS, the messages are sent and responses received in digital format, cutting transmission time to micro-seconds. This greatly increases the amount of information which can be exchanged. Voice communications on the

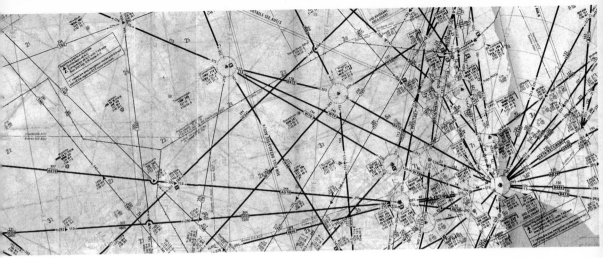

Above:
Chart AUS/3 shows airway A576 from Derby across Alice Springs to Bindook, prior to the approach to Sydney.

Left:
The Sydney area chart shows the routing from Bindook to Sydney over the Blue Mountain range passing Camden and Bankstown.

company frequencies tend to be one or two per flight. On the other hand ACARS generates over 20 messages per flight with the information being of a much higher quality. This information can be displayed either on a VDU or in print-out form while the ground-based and airborne computers are communicating directly.

British Airways began to take advantage of these new systems towards the end of 1988 in its Airbus A320 fleet, and continued it with the introduction of the Boeing 747-400. British Airways also had a unique approach to ACARS in the decision to retrofit its entire modern fleet, leaving out the older 747s and the BAC 1-11 fleet due to the anticipated disposal of these aircraft.

British Airways was largely engineering driven in adopting ACARS because the airline realised that there was enough computing power in the air to carry out performance monitoring, which could previously only be done on the ground. The results can be downlinked in real time, whereas previously the information could take up to five days to be analysed — possibly too late for any remedial action. Using engine health monitors (EHM) trouble can be anticipated and a solution devised by computer. This improves safety and cost savings in terms of mechanical damage and aircraft downtime. Preventive maintenance — the insurance against breakdowns — can be planned and targeted with greater precision, thereby reducing costs whilst maintaining safety levels. Any defective parts can be detected in flight and a replacement can be available for the arrival of the aircraft at its next destination if it is simply change of a line replaceable unit (LRU). An engineer sitting at his desk at London Heathrow can download data from any aircraft flying within VHF range of the remote ground stations, where appropriate.

The arrival of ACARS has been an evolutionary process with the capability of the new generation digital airliners and development of the suitable software. Modification of earlier aircraft is not a major problem in hardware terms, but the major challenge is to programme the older aircraft into the overall fleet maintenance schedule.

Because of the higher intelligence levels of the latest equipment, British Airways will gain greater benefits, especially as new methods are tried and work, increasing the usage dramatically. Aircom, as the system is known with British Airways, can lead to faster turn-arounds, more efficient maintenance and better aircraft utilisation. It can also bring about further passenger service improvements.

To meet busy departure slots for the airways, the aircraft needs to have the doors closed and push-back on schedule, or face delays of up to two hours in the worst conditions. One of the most common reasons for missed slots is the late arrival of load sheets due to last minute passengers or cargo. Until the captain has seen and approved the load sheet, the doors cannot be closed for departure. Often the taxi time to the departure point can be quite lengthy and, if the aircraft is equipped with on board Aircom printer, the captain can receive the document while he waits in the take off queue, and certainly before the take-off clearance is given.

'Oooitimes' are monitored in real time from switches located in all the active areas, including landing lights, radio altimeter and flaps. This allows British Airways to have a 'nearly there' signal, which advises when the aircraft is established on the final approach. This allows for the most efficient use of ramp personnel and equipment, who would never need to arrive too early or be late.

Air traffic control clearances which are often long and complex, will be passed by ACARS to a flightdeck printer, reducing the chances of error, and the VHF clutter caused by the clearance and read back. The progressive introduction of the more efficient two crew flightdeck operation requires a reduction in the time spent on the radio during one of the busiest periods. Routine information such as the aerodrome terminal information service (ATIS) could also be received by the crew and read at the appropriate time, together with a last minute update on the weather at the destination and alternates.

To overcome the limitations of the existing ground stations on the VHF link, ACARS is now being satellite-linked to cover areas of the world not covered by the ground stations. This is particularly helpful over remote areas of land or the long oceanic routes. The major disadvantage with Satcom over the ground-based systems, is the 10-fold increase in installation costs. The advantage is, however, that linking into the satellite system will give the airline global coverage, providing a complete international telephone service to its passengers. It may be that very many of the future high-yield passengers, who are targeted for these improvements, will choose the airline according to the telephone service and the other benefits. Digital downlinks via satellite will give access to computer reservation systems providing rapid confirmation for onward travel, hotel reservations and hire-car bookings.

The immediate functions for ACARS with British Airways cover company operations, maintenance and flight operations. The company operations include flight progress, delays, diversions, weather, fuel and weight and balance. As already discussed maintenance data is received on engine monitoring, line maintenance and overall maintenance planning. Flight operations information will record flight time logging and help plan crew scheduling.

Longer term functions already in development will expand flight operations and add cabin management with more to follow. Typical of the flight operations information will be oceanic clearances, track progress, replacement of repetitive weather broadcast and ATIS material. Cabin management will include catering needs, transfer assistance, local information and passenger messages. A revolution in the efficient operation of an air transport system.

Although there are a number of routine tasks to be dealt with on the long cruise such as keeping the flight logs up to date, position reports up date on the radio and maintaining a knowledge of the weather and operation of the aircraft systems, this is the time when the crew can relax a little, but not to the extent of reading a book. The captain can make a walk-about of the passenger cabins, not only for exercise, but also as part of the customer relations. However, one crew member must be strapped in one of the pilots seats all the time the aircraft is airborne, and two crew during any of the busy periods, such as departure and arrival. On the flight to Sydney over or near land masses, there tends to be a continual need to keep up with the reporting points, but over long oceanic flights, radio aids are less available and, therefore, the aircraft will fly a great circle route between way points as the shortest distance available.

For these long routine flights, a system has been devised to monitor crew alertness. If no crew action is detected, such as radio calls, autopilot functions, systems monitoring or FMC operation, over a specified time, a message comes up on the EICAS screen. If a crew member acts to erase the message, the system is satisfied. If no action is taken to erase the message, the system will cause it to be flashed, and after a further period of time oral warning will alert the crew into action.

As we approach the Australian coast line near Derby, we have reached the cruising altitude of 37,000ft which saves us about four tonnes of fuel and makes us 10min ahead of schedule. Our track is 120°, we are cruising at M. 0.85 and our ground speed is 526kt. Flying high over the arid vast mid-Australian deserts with Alice Springs about the mid-point, thunderstorms are reported in the Sydney area as expected.

As we approach the top of descent point, Capt Calcutt elects to make the landing, taking control from about 1,000ft above the runway on the approach, while Dick Norriss will fly the aircraft down the descent. Dick selects 118.5 on the VHF and calls, 'Speedbird one one request runway 34' which is granted. This gives a curved

Right:
The Sydney approach chart for runway 34.

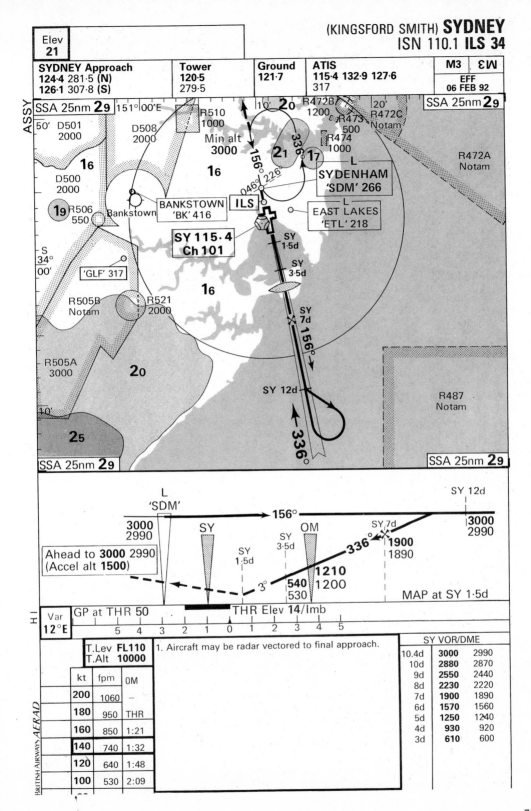

Elev 21					M3	ƎW
SYDNEY Approach 124·4 281·5 (N) 126·1 307·8 (S)	**Tower** 120·5 279·5	**Ground** 121·7	**ATIS** 115·4 132·9 127·6 317		EFF 06 FEB 92	

Chart detail (plan view):

- ASSY
- SSA 25nm **29**
- 151°00'E
- R510 1000, Min alt **3000**, 16
- D508 2000, D501 2000, 50'
- R472B 1200, 20, R472C Notam, R473 500, R474 1000, R472A Notam, 20
- 336°, 21, 17, L SYDENHAM 'SDM' 266
- 156°, 226°, 046°
- **ILS**, BANKSTOWN 'BK' 416, Bankstown, R506 550, 19
- **SY 115·4 Ch 101**, L EAST LAKES 'ETL' 218
- D500 2000, 16
- 'GLF' 317, S 34°00'
- SY 1·5d, SY 3·5d
- R505B Notam, R521 2000, 16
- SY 7d, 156°
- R505A 3000, 2o, SY 12d, 336°
- R487 Notam
- SSA 25nm **29**
- 10', 2s
- Var **12°E**
- H I

Profile view:

- L 'SDM'
- 156°, 3000 2990
- Ahead to **3000** 2990 (Accel alt **1500**)
- SY, OM
- SY 1·5d, SY 3·5d, SY 7d
- 336°, **1900** 1890
- **1210**, **540** 530, **1200**
- 3°, MAP at SY 1·5d
- SY 12d, **3000** 2990
- GP at THR 50, THR Elev **14**/1mb
- 5 4 3 2 1 0 1 2 3 4 5

T.Lev **FL110** T.Alt **10000**	1. Aircraft may be radar vectored to final approach.	SY VOR/DME		
		10.4d	**3000**	2990
		10d	**2880**	2870
		9d	**2550**	2440
		8d	**2230**	2220
		7d	**1900**	1890
		6d	**1570**	1560
		5d	**1250**	1240
		4d	**930**	920
		3d	**610**	600

kt	fpm	OM
200	1060	–
180	950	THR
160	850	1:21
140	740	1:32
120	640	1:48
100	530	2:09

BRITISH AIRWAYS *AERAD*

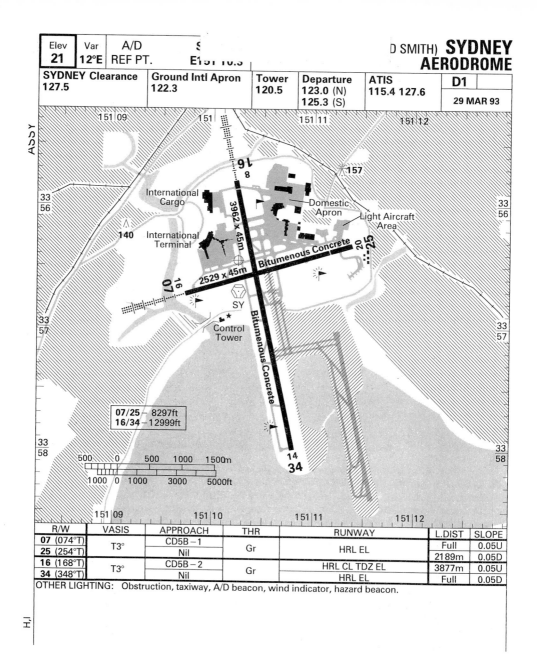

| Elev **21** | Var **12°E** | A/D REF PT. | S~~E151 10.3~~ | | | D SMITH) **SYDNEY AERODROME** |

SYDNEY Clearance **127.5**	Ground Intl Apron **122.3**	Tower **120.5**	Departure **123.0** (N) **125.3** (S)	ATIS **115.4 127.6**	**D1**
					29 MAR 93

07/25 — 8297ft
16/34 — 12999ft

R/W	VASIS	APPROACH	THR	RUNWAY		L.DIST	SLOPE
07 (074°T)	T3°	CD5B – 1	Gr	HRL EL		Full	0.05U
25 (254°T)		Nil				2189m	0.05D
16 (168°T)	T3°	CD5B – 2	Gr	HRL CL TDZ EL		3877m	0.05U
34 (348°T)		Nil		HRL EL		Full	0.05D

OTHER LIGHTING: Obstruction, taxiway, A/D beacon, wind indicator, hazard beacon.

approach over Botany Bay and close to over the spot where Capt Cook made his first landfall in Australia.

The crew run through their descent briefing and we can see the build up of the thunderclouds on either side of our path, although checking on the colour weather radar display on the EFIS, our proposed route looks clear. The dark red of the hazardous centres of the thunderstorms show up brightly, the storm that was over Sydney gradually moving away to the north beyond the harbour and out into the Pacific Ocean. Our procedure will take us to the Bindook beacon and then straight in on runway 34. The DME shows us as 70nm from the VOR at Parkes which itself is 27min from touchdown and we are asked to slow down to M 0.83 to give separation from an aircraft in front of us.

In between the descent activity, we made a call on the company frequency that we are to land on 34 and we have three passengers who will need wheelchair assistance. We are allocated stand 21.

At 09.05 GMT, Dick Norriss takes control, as the crew tighten up their harnesses ready for the arrival. We tune into the Sydney ATIS where information C is being broadcast, which gives 7 octas of cloud at 3,400ft, wind 020 10-15kt, temperature 21°C, Cu Nimbus in the area and the QNH 1,003.

'Speedbird one one — heading one one five.'

'One one five, Speedbird one one,' we confirm.

'Speedbird one one, descent flight level 280, track 115.'

'Speedbird one one, leaving 370 for 280.'

As we commence our descent, the time is 09.10 GMT and we are approaching the darkness which is beginning to come across Sydney as the sun sets in the west. Our target speed for the final approach was 155kt.

'Speedbird one one descending to level 190.' We heard a call which confirmed we are being followed by Gulf Air 148.

'Speedbird one one contact Sydney Control 123.4.' The Sydney controllers speak very precise RT procedures no doubt due to the many foreign aircraft in their airspace, to avoid any misunderstanding.

'Sydney, Speedbird one one passing 245 heading 112.'

'Speedbird one one, airspeed 275, descend FL120.' The time is 09.16 GMT.

'Speedbird one one descend 7000 (QNH) 1,003.' We acknowledge.

Left:
The Sydney Aerodrome chart.

'Sydney, Speedbird one one turning left to 072 15,000ft descending.'

The time is 09.20 and it is now dark as we track across the Blue Mountain range and see the vast spread of lights of Sydney and its western suburbs. At least on the flightdeck it is possible to see the surroundings, even though it is now dark. Your compiler is frequently frustrated by the helpful messages from the flightdeck which highlight certain interesting features, which can always be viewed from the opposite side of the aircraft to where one is seated.

'Speedbird one one, contact approach one, two six decimal one, good-day.'

'Speedbird one one passing 7,000 with Charlie.'

'Speedbird one one 5,000 left base runway 34, five miles to run.'

'Speedbird one one, steer one zero zero.'

'Speedbird one one descend 3,000ft. As we approach towards Botany Bay with the lights of Sydney ahead, it is difficult to pick out the runway lights. Flap 1 and flap 5 (degrees) are selected.

'Speedbird one one 3,000 060.'

'2,000 Speedbird one one.' Flaps 10.

'Speedbird one one 010 clear for finals.'

'Clear for finals, Speedbird one one.'

We select undercarriage down, flaps 20 and start the landing checks. The flaps are lowered a further five degrees as the landing checks are completed and we cross the outer marker. The captain takes control at 1,000ft and we see the runway lights beginning to fill the cockpit windscreens.

'Speedbird one one, clear land runway 34.' We acknowledge and make our touchdown smoothly at 09.35 GMT, or 20.35 local time. We slow to 80kt on the runway with the sea on either side.

'Speedbird one one, cross the intersection (of the two runways) and vacate, call ground on 121.7.'

'Speedbird one one next left and then right for Bay 21.'

As we continue rolling the first officer retracts the flaps, switches the weather radar off and completes the landing checks while we vacate the runway. As we move slowly along the designated taxiway towards the terminal, we are asked to hold pending the removal of an aircraft tug blocking the way. With this removed, we are cleared to taxi to Bay 21, which is right in the corner of the terminal building apron. We come to a halt at 09.44 GMT some 21hr after our departure from Heathrow, and everyone prepares to disembark into the temperate Sydney summer evening.

Above:
A British Airways' 747-400 touching down on Runway 16 at Sydney. *Andrew Briggs*

This picture:
A British Airways' 747-400 landing at Sydney on Runway 16 with the city skyline in the background. *Andrew Briggs*

Above:
A British Airways' 747-400 is seen taxying from runway 16 at Sydney. *Andrew Briggs*

Top:
A British Airways 747-400 on taxiway A at Sydney Airport.

Right:
The Sydney Ramp Chart shows stand 21 in the corner nearest the terminal on Apron 1.

Above:
A 747-400 turning into the International Apron 1 at Sydney.

Below:
A 747-400 of BA is pictured on the International Apron 1 at Sydney.

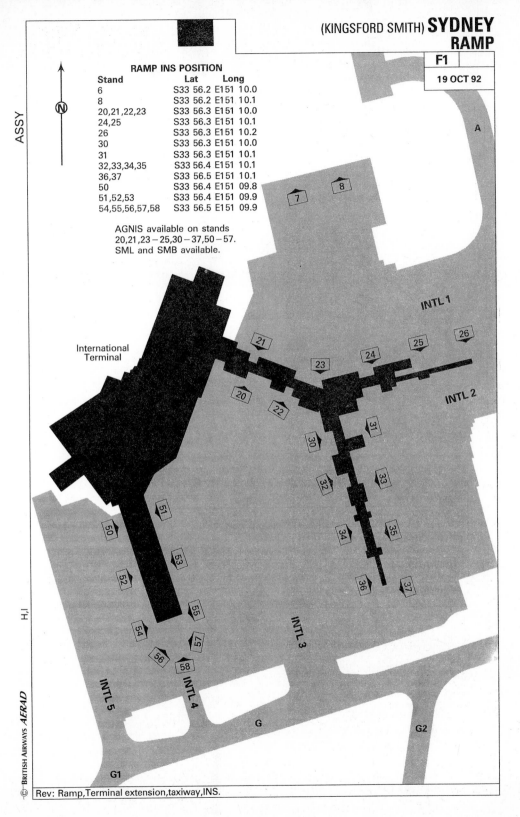

ASSY

RAMP INS POSITION

Stand	Lat	Long
6	S33 56.2	E151 10.0
8	S33 56.2	E151 10.1
20,21,22,23	S33 56.3	E151 10.0
24,25	S33 56.3	E151 10.1
26	S33 56.3	E151 10.2
30	S33 56.3	E151 10.0
31	S33 56.3	E151 10.1
32,33,34,35	S33 56.4	E151 10.1
36,37	S33 56.5	E151 10.1
50	S33 56.4	E151 09.8
51,52,53	S33 56.4	E151 09.9
54,55,56,57,58	S33 56.5	E151 09.9

AGNIS available on stands
20,21,23 – 25,30 – 37,50 – 57.
SML and SMB available.

A

7   8

INTL 1

International
Terminal

21   25   26
      24
23

20   22   31

30

INTL 2

32   33

51   34   35

50   53

52   36   37

55

54   57   INTL 3

56

58

INTL 5   INTL 4   G   G2

H,I

G1

© BRITISH AIRWAYS *AERAD*

Rev: Ramp,Terminal extension,taxiway,INS.

Top:
British Airways' 747-400 turning into its stand.

Above:
British Airways' 747-400 on stand at Sydney Airport.

6. British Airways & the Boeing 747-400

The first Boeing 747 Jumbo jet was rolled out at Seattle on 30 September 1968. The new aircraft represented a dramatic increase in the passenger carrying capacity over the earlier Boeing 707s and Douglas DC-8s. Twenty years later, with the original company-owned prototype still airworthy, the world fleet of 747s had carried 846.7 million passengers, flown 11,921 million miles and logged 23.61 million hours of revenue flying since entering service with Pan Am on 21 January 1970. Many tales were told in the early days of Jumbo jets flying across the north Atlantic only half full of passengers, as a result of the sudden increase in capacity, but, today, on the world's major trunk routes it is rare to see a Jumbo jet operating with a significant number of empty seats. Despite this, the heavy discounting of fares to try to fill the seats, often results in a loss due to insufficient yield.

In May 1985, Boeing announced the development of the new model 747-400, an advanced long-range version of the existing 747-300. Although it looked superficially like other Boeing 747s, it had a number of significant advances to not only improve the performance, but also update the technology in line with much of the competition. Boeing has always been conservative in its approach to new technology, insisting that it should only be introduced if it pays for itself.

The 747-400 was an advanced long-range version of the earlier 747-300 and it replaced, in due course, all the previous models. Boeing ended production of the 747-200 in November 1991 with the delivery of the 393rd example, a freighter, to Nippon Air Cargo of Japan. This marked the end of a 21-year production run. The company had delivered a total of 223 all-passenger -200s, 73 freighters, 78 Combis, 13

The Boeing 747-400 production line at Everett. *Boeing*

convertibles, four USAF E-4Bs and two US Presidential aircraft. Boeing had taken orders for 1,148 of all types of this classic passenger airliner including 205 -100s, 45 747SPs and 81 -300s.

The improvements to the 747-400 include more powerful 58,000lb (258kN) thrust engines with a choice of the GE CF6-80C2, Pratt & Whitney PW4056 or Rolls-Royce RB211-524G, a modern two-crew digital flightdeck, more flexible cabin configurations, increased range and better fuel economy.

Design of the original Boeing 747 was little influenced by the airlines which had some apprehension about how they were going to be able to operate and maintain this giant new aircraft. However, Boeing have learned in the intervening period and consulted 14 major airlines in helping to establish the design of the -400.

In the flight development programme the first aircraft to fly was Pratt & Whitney-powered, the second General Electric and the third aircraft Rolls-Royce. Certification and deliveries commenced in the first half of 1989. The basic price of these aircraft was in the order of $120 million.

Above:
Another 747-400 rolls of the Boeing production line at Everett. *Boeing*

Above right:
The first Boeing 747-400 made its maiden flight on 29 April 1988. *Boeing*

The major distinguishing mark of the 747-400 over the 747-300, with its similarly stretched upper-deck, are the winglets. These 6ft winglets have a sweep back of 60° and are canted out at an angle of 22°. They are metal sparred with carbon skin and are mounted on wingtips extended by 12ft span overall. These winglets, along with drag reducing improvements around the wing to fuselage fairing, give a seven percent fuel consumption reduction per passenger mile. The -400 can carry over 400 passengers more than 7,000nm, which is 1,000nm further than the -300.

Although the main wing structure and the control surfaces are similar to the earlier versions, by using the new lighter high strength aluminium alloys as developed for the 757 and 767 a weight saving of some 6,000lb has been

achieved. The replacement of steel brakes with carbon brakes and new wider wheels with low-profile tyres has saved a further 1,800lb.

As already noted, a major internal change is the configuration of the flightdeck for two-pilot operation with the flight engineers systems placed in the roof between the pilots. The major flight information is displayed across six 8in by 8in glass screens. Improvements include digital electronic engine control — known as power by wire — fuel in the tailplane, plumbing for up to 26 toilets and crew rest areas.

Boeing's initial approach to the -400, particularly on the flightdeck, was minimum change including the retention of the electro-mechanical instruments. This was supported by Cathay Pacific, one of the launch customers, to minimise retraining. However, in 1985, the concept changed due to pressure from other customers who were experiencing the improved technology fitted to the Boeing 757 and 767 twins, as well as with the Airbus product range. As a result, Boeing formed a consultative group of the major airline prospects including British Airways, Cathay, KLM, Lufthansa, Qantas, Singapore Airlines and Northwest. These airlines were, therefore, able to influence Boeing to update the aircraft with the latest digital avionics, which had advanced through about three generations since the early 747. This would allow the adoption of the new features such as collision avoidance, datalink, wind shear warning and 4D navigation.

The initial Boeing response was to use the 757/767 technology, but the more advanced Airbus A320 was entering service, providing a practical driving force for further improved EFIS displays, giving fault warnings and corrective actions. Costs had to be a major parameter in the change programme, especially as the 747-400 was not a clean sheet of paper. As a result, the digital 747-400 emerged as a very efficient update of the 20-year old basic design and, although it was very different to step straight into and fly, the transition was not too demanding. The converting pilots learned quickly to change scan and cues in the apparently roomier flightdeck. The main response was how had they managed in the past!

The resultant two-pilot flightdeck has all the primary flight, engine and systems information displayed on six big interchangeable glass

screens. Each pilot has the two screens side by side, unlike the 757/767 where they are one above the other. The captain's left screen is the primary flight display showing horizon, attitude, airspeed, altitude, vertical speed and heading. The captain's right-hand screen is the navigation display, replacing the old moving map. The screens are reversed for the first officer. On the navigation display, the aircraft symbol can be located in the centre to allow the pilot to view all around in busy terminal areas where air traffic instructions may involve tight manoeuvres. The ND display has four modes with approach, VOR, map and flight plan with either the full compass rose or an enlarged quadrant. Full colour weather radar pictures can be superimposed for avoidance of hazardous conditions. If a PFD fails, the information can be immediately switched to the ND panel, with the other pair still operating. Basic electro-mechanical instruments are fitted in the unlikely event of a total failure of all the flight and navigation displays.

The two middle screens positioned one above the other are known as EICAS (engine indication and crew alerting system) similar to the 757/767. Primary engine data is displayed generally on the upper screen, together with aircraft status information. The lower EICAS display presents the engine data or systems pages. Should a fault occur the systems give warnings and cautions and the crew use the quick reference checklists to follow the correct procedures. Each system can survive multiple failures provided that the correct procedures are followed, not only to cover safety but also to facilitate despatch.

The new Honeywell (Sperry) flight management system (FMC) takes a maximum of three seconds to complete a calculation, which would take up to 20sec on the earlier 747. British Airways contributed towards the thrust lever control by the FMC rather than a separate computer. The FMC also provides an answer to the previously mentioned 4D navigation problem, such as when air traffic ask the pilot to make a certain way point at a different altitude. Each way point has a time attached to it, bringing in the fourth dimension.

The Collins autopilot hardware is basically the same as the 757/767, but is fitted with new software. An important new facility on this full digital triplex system is Altitude Intervention, which can handle an unexpected change of height caused by air traffic instruction without the crew recalculating the flight plan. The work done by British Airways and the CAA on the autoland system of the Boeing 747 has contributed to the smooth introduction of the -400 to Cat IIIB autoland giving no decision height and a visibility of 75m. We have already discussed engine failure on take-off in an earlier chapter but, if there is an engine failure on the automatic approach, the autopilot controls the rudder. The 747-400 rudder has an increase of five degrees movement to 30° over earlier 747s. New rudder actuators decrease the runway minimum control speed by 10kt.

The 747-400 can be powered by engines from all three big turbofan manufacturers. All of these have achieved a high level of reliability due to years of commercial service, at the same time competing to give the greatest thrust for the greatest economy. All three engines have reduced fuel burn by 5-10% over the last decade and all have commonalty with the 767 installation. All three engine types are capable of full-authority digital engine control (Fadec); the Rolls-Royce RB211-524L was the first of this engine type. However, British Airways have selected the 58,000lb-thrust -524G engines, in order to provide commonality with their 767-300 fleet. The other main installed power unit is the all new Pratt & Whitney Canada PW901A auxiliary power unit which first ran in 1987 and was specified for the 747-400. It burns 40% less fuel while working more effectively, and has automatic starting, monitoring and shutdown. The APU drives two generators; it can be used in the air or on the ground and is more environmentally-friendly than other APUs of similar size.

Within the systems the hydraulics are essen-

tially unchanged apart from refinements to match the new design, the working pressure being at a traditional 3,000lb/sq in. Electrical supply is from four engine-driven 90kVa Sundstrand generators and the digital database wiring is reduced significantly from earlier 747s. The automatic fuel system has the option of a 3,300 US gall tailplane fuel tank, giving another 350nm range. Fuel management and measurement is all automatic.

The five-truck — four main and one nose — 18-wheel undercarriage architecture is unchanged from previous models. However, the wheels are two inches greater in diameter to house the more substantial carbon brake packs, but the overall wheel diameter is maintained through using lower profile tyres.

For an airline customer probably the most important feature of any aircraft is the cabin. The 747-400 cabin has been restyled to give an even wider look and the overhead bins have more than doubled in volume, taking even the most stubborn carry-on bag. The main deck can seat 3-4-3 with a pair of 20in aisles and a total of 110in headroom. The cabin trim and furnishings

Left:
The winglet of the new 747-400 silhouetted against the sunset. *Boeing*

Below:
This pilotless Boeing 747-400 digital cockpit is apparently at nearly 31,000ft. This simulator shot shows the Efis panels and cockpit layout. *Boeing*

are all to the latest fireworthiness standards and the seats designed to withstand 16g loads which is approaching the limitations of human endurance. Smoke extraction and air circulation has been improved by increasing the air-conditioning zones from three to five, with a higher ventilation rate.

The basic structural design of the 747 has had its testing moments, although structural failure has never been catastrophic. In the new model, Boeing have strengthened all areas which have been prone to cracks in the past, the large front end having thicker frames, skins and doublers to avoid the expensive repair schemes. Corrosion protection has been further improved by white epoxy paint in the under floor areas, particular attention being made in the areas below and around the toilets and galleys. The 747-400 economic design life is set at 60,000hr, 20,000 flights or 20 years. So far some 100 of the early 747s have clocked up 60,000hr and are still going strong with regular monitoring of the structure to ensure its integrity.

The maintenance of the 747-400 is made easier with its digital database replacing miles of wiring. The central maintenance computer (CMC) is located on the console between the pilots which co-ordinates Bite interpretation of all the systems centrally, giving faults in plain English on the screen. Using this system ground engineers will be able to locate and fix faults promptly and, in the air, it will keep the air crew informed.

The first Boeing 747-400 shared the limelight with the first 737-400, when they were both formally rolled out on the same day in late January 1988. The 737-400 roll-out was at the Boeing narrow-body aircraft facility at Renton in the morning, followed by the debut of the 747-400 at the massive Everett facility 27 miles away, in the afternoon. Orders for the 747-400 then stood at 117 with options on a further 54 from 17 airlines. The orders were worth a total of more than $12 billion. Northwest was the launch customer with 10 aircraft on order powered by the Pratt & Whitney engines, which were fitted to the first aircraft to fly.

On 25 March 1988 Rolls-Royce were awarded the certificate of airworthiness for the 58,000lb-thrust RB211-524G by the CAA. This approval was in time for Rolls-Royce to ship the first set of engines to Boeing for installation in the third 747-400 to start its development programme.

Despite delays due to integration problems of

Above:
The first-class cabin of the Boeing 747-400. *Boeing*

Overleaf:
The first two 747-400s on formal handover to British Airways at Boeing Field. *Boeing*

the new two-man crew avionics the first 747-400 made its maiden flight on 29 April 1988. The flight lasted 2hr 26min and reached a speed of M 0.7 at an altitude of 20,000ft. As the development programme progressed with the first GE CF6-80C2 joining the testing, the first Rolls-Royce-powered -400 made its maiden flight on 28 August 1988 to become the third aircraft in the development trio. This aircraft was in the colours of Cathay Pacific, the launch customer of this version. Sales of the Rolls-Royce RB211-powered aircraft total 65 for Cathay, BA, Qantas, Air New Zealand and the International Lease Finance Corporation (ILFC). At this time, BA had firm orders for 19 of the type with options on a further 12 aircraft, worth a potential investment of near $4 billion.

By October 1988, Boeing were admitting delays in the early 747-400 programme due to receiving more orders than expected, extensive customer configuration differences and certification of the aircraft with three different engine types. British Airways and Qantas had elected for a common standard to allow use of each other's aircraft where appropriate to reduce costs. To help reduce delays the aircraft were being flight tested seven days a week in an effort

Above:
The business-class cabin of the Boeing 747-400.
Boeing

Below:
A British Airways' 747-400 lands at Boeing Field after a test flight. *Boeing*

to recover time lost early in the programme and to try and achieve certification and deliveries by the end of the year. The maiden flight of the first aircraft had been delayed by six weeks due to late delivery by some Boeing suppliers and modifications to the new electronic systems. The other aircraft were also late in joining the development programme, but the absence of any significant problems during the testing were expected to help reduce overall delays. The test aircraft were averaging 65hr a month with peaks of 90hr a month early in the programme. The testing of the wing extensions, winglets, and tailplane fuel tank raised no major problems but, in early October 1988, a major portion of the testing centred on the performance of the digital avionics and the refinement of the computer software.

By mid-October, four aircraft were participating in the test programme, with more than 500 flight-test hours logged in 180 flights. Flutter clearance and performance evaluation of all three engine types had been completed, and current testing involved low speed aerodynamic performance and autopilot development leading to autoland trails. Fuel economy was also to be looked at and throughout the flight envelope the handling qualities were equal to or better than the earlier 747s. Other work included gathering data for simulator use and the compilation of the aircraft flight manuals. During the flight development programme major milestones achieved included a non-stop flight of more than 14hr and a new world record for the heaviest take-off by a civilian aircraft at 892,450lb.

The 747-400 achieved its FAA certification with Pratt & Whitney engines on 9 January, 1989. It had taken a month longer than programme allowed due to the testing of the technical advances in the new development. The eight and a half month test programme totalled 2,600hr of which about half was in the air using four aircraft. Certification work continued with the GE and Rolls-Royce engines. The first delivery was made to Northwest on 26 January — within one month of the original planned schedule. Total deliveries for 1989 were expected to cover 57 aircraft, more than doubling the production rate to 4.75 per month. The CAA in Britain issued the type certificate for the Rolls-Royce powered 747-400 in June 1989, but gave two years for Boeing to comply with the full European Joint Airworthiness standards with respect to upper-deck floor strength and venting in the event of a major decompression. Boeing had hoped to delay this further due to the derivative nature of the basic aircraft, but this was not acceptable to the European authorities.

In early July, British Airways crews commenced training on their first 747-400, G-BNLA although teams from nearly every department within the airline had been involved for almost three years in preparing for the introduction of the new fleet. British Airways had placed its initial order for 16 aircraft on 15 August 1986, later adding three more. This took the value of the total order, options and spares to $4.5 billion.

The first 747-400 for British Airways made its maiden flight at the end of May and was used to achieve the CAA certification up to the end of

June when it was formally accepted by British Airways. The crew training included the senior pilots and training captains, the initial cabin crews and the engineering support team ready for its introduction into commercial service.

In ceremonies at Boeing Field, Lord King, the then Chairman of British Airways, accepted the first two 747-400s — G-BNLA, *City of London*, and G-BNLB, *City of Cardiff* — on 26 July 1989. The $125 million 386-seat aircraft would bring all destinations on the BA worldwide network, except Australia and New Zealand, within non-stop range of London. These two aircraft were delivered simultaneously to Heathrow, landing on the parallel runways on 27 July 1989 — the 40th anniversary of the maiden flight of the de Havilland Comet, the world's first commercial jet airliner. The Comet had been introduced by

Left:
The first two Boeing 747-400 aircraft for British Airways. *BA*

Below:
The first Boeing 747-400, G-BNLA, touches down on runway 27L at London Heathrow on its delivery flight. *BA*

BOAC in April 1952. The original Comet 1 could carry 36 passengers over about 2,000 miles, compared with the 747-400 which carries 386 passengers and 16 tonnes of cargo over distances of up to 8,000 miles at very much increased speed.

Only one day after its delivery, the first 747-400 entered scheduled passenger service with British Airways, operating flight BA 219 to Philadelphia and Pittsburgh. This inaugurated a new era in long-haul flying. The aircraft were used initially on the shorter North Atlantic routes to build up crew and operational experience before starting the ultra long-haul routes to Singapore and Sydney. These services were planned to start at the end of August when sufficient aircraft were delivered. Initially, the aircraft operated two weekly one-stop services from London to Australia via Singapore, cutting the journey time to Asia by two hours. From Singapore, the flights head to Sydney and then on to Brisbane or Melbourne. By the beginning of 1990, the frequency of this flight increased to four a week.

In July, 1990, British Airways signed their largest ever contract with Boeing for up to 33

additional 747-400 aircraft worth around $6.4 billion. The order included 21 firm orders, seven of which were the conversion of previous options, with options on another 12, taking total commitments to 53 aircraft. At that time, 13 of the new aircraft had entered service with British Airways. Total orders for the -400 had reached, by this time, 335 with 76 delivered.

In September 1991, British Airways were granted Cat IIIB autoland clearance for the 747-400s. This permits a decision height at touch down and zero visibility. For practical purposes, with the cloudbase at ground level, BA have set a limit of 100m to enable taxying off the runway. The certification was achieved by monitoring autolandings on the BA and Cathay 747-400s, using 440 approaches. Data on 176 of these had been printed out on the newly fitted aircraft condition monitoring system (ACMS), clearance also being obtained for three-engined approaches to the same minima. The benefits to the airline is greater crew confidence in the final destination or diversion decision as well as saving the costs of accommodation up to £100,000 for the crew and passengers on a diversion. The passengers also have a much greater probability of arriving on time at their expected destination, even if they have difficulty with surface transport on arrival.

British Airways is therefore committed to the latest generation of long-range high-technology transport aircraft taking passengers in improved comfort to their intended destination in shorter times. Not only is there an improvement in the cruising speed, but the elimination of unwanted technical stops will certainly be an advantage. The advanced technology will give greater reliability and redundancy, once again cutting down on delays which can be so frustrating whether the passengers have urgent deadlines to meet, or just plain leisure when long airport delays can reduce all the benefits of a good holiday.

British Airways' Boeing 747-400 G-BNLC. *BA*